S0-BCU-969

Black Men in Higher Education

Black Men in Higher Education bridges theory to practice in order to better prepare practitioners in their efforts to increase the success of Black male students in colleges and universities. In this comprehensive but manageable text, leading researchers J. Luke Wood and Robert T. Palmer highlight the current status of Black men in higher education and review relevant research literature and theory on their experiences in various postsecondary education contexts. The authors also provide and contextualize innovative, actionable strategies and solutions to help institutions increase the participation and success of Black male college students. The most recent addition to the *Key Issues on Diverse College Students* series, this volume is a valuable resource for student affairs and higher education professionals to better serve Black men in higher education.

J. Luke Wood is Associate Professor of Community College Leadership at San Diego State University, USA.

Robert T. Palmer is Associate Professor of Student Affairs Administration at the State University of New York, Binghamton, USA.

Black Men in Higher Education

A Guide to Ensuring Student Success

J. Luke Wood and
Robert T. Palmer

Routledge
Taylor & Francis Group

NEW YORK AND LONDON

First published 2015
by Routledge
711 Third Avenue, New York, NY 10017

and by Routledge
2 Park Square, Milton Park, Abingdon, Oxon, OX14 4RN

Routledge is an imprint of the Taylor & Francis Group, an informa business

Library of Congress Cataloging in Publication Data
Wood, J. Luke, 1982–
Black men in higher education: a guide to ensuring student success/
J. Luke Wood, Robert T. Palmer.
    pages cm.—(Key issues on diverse college students)
    Includes bibliographical references and index.
    1. African American men—Education (Higher)
    2. African American men—Social conditions.
    3. African American college students. I. Palmer, Robert T. II. Title.
    LC2781.W66 2014
    378.1′982996073—dc23   2014016773

ISBN: 978-0-415-71484-6 (hbk)
ISBN: 978-0-415-71485-3 (pbk)
ISBN: 978-1-315-88235-2 (ebk)

Typeset in Perpetua and Bell Gothic
by Florence Production Ltd, Stoodleigh, Devon, UK

Printed and bound in the United States of America by Publishers Graphics,
LLC on sustainably sourced paper.

J. Luke Wood dedicates this book to Ernie Micheli, who taught him the importance of affirmation, high expectations, and authentic care.

Robert T. Palmer dedicates this book to his mentors and friends in the academy, who have inspired him to be resilient and focus on succeeding in every endeavor.

Contents

Foreword

> If, as scholars of higher education, we wish to produce knowledge to improve student success, we cannot ignore that practitioners play a significant role. More specifically, if our goal is to do scholarship that makes a difference in the lives of students whom higher education has been least successful in educating (e.g., racially marginalized groups and the poor), we have to expand the scholarship on student success and take into account the influence of practitioners—positively and negatively. If we continue to concentrate only on what students accomplished or failed to accomplish when they were in high school and what they do or fail to do once they enter college, our understanding of success will be flawed, as well as incomplete.

The quote above comes from Dr. Estela Bensimon's 2007 presidential address to the Association to the Study of Higher Education. Bensimon's remarks are a compelling reminder of the need for educators to reframe the ways in which they conceptualize student success and to reconsider the strategies they employ to facilitate it within institutions of higher education. Perhaps no group could be better served by a calibrated concept of student success than Black men from whom the gains and outcomes of higher education have always been elusive. It is in this vein of scholarship—that which calls for greater institutional responsibility and accountability for Black male student success—that this book is written. Simply stated, efforts to redress the persistent and gross disparities between Black men and other groups in postsecondary access, engagement, and success must begin with the question: "What are we doing (or not doing) as a program, department, college, or institution to ensure that Black men have the experiences and opportunities they need to be successful?"

As I reflect upon my time as an undergraduate at Loyola Marymount University, I recall entering college with what some may perceive to be "deficits." I was educated in an under-resourced urban high school, I had a less than desirable SAT score, I had not taken advanced placement courses, and my parents were not college graduates. Fortunately, I enrolled at an institution that was staffed by educators who were less concerned with what I wasn't and more concerned with what I had the potential to be. Perhaps more important, they took the time to get to know me, recognized my strengths, and provided the capital I needed to be successful—all while consistently upholding high expectations of me. Never did I feel incapable. As a result, I achieved goals and reached heights I never thought were attainable. Unfortunately, it seems as though the experience I had as an undergraduate is the exception rather than the rule for Black men in U. S. higher education. A cursory glance at the published literature and news stories will reveal alarming patterns of inequity and despair for this population. In fact, one could easily conclude that success for Black men on college and university campuses is relegated to the hardwood or gridiron, not a lecture hall or a lab.

Black Men in Higher Education is a clarion call to those of us in the academy to assume greater responsibility for Black men's success. When a Black male considers withdrawing from our institutions prior to earning a degree, reports being targeted in a racially hostile interaction, or says "I don't feel like I belong here," we should feel *personally* obligated to do something about it. Anything less is a failure on *our* part, not the student's.

Black Men in Higher Education is a significant contribution to the student success literature in several notable respects. First, it is one of the few books that accounts for what happens to Black males at all the critical junctures of their educational journeys, beginning in PreK through higher education. Second, as noted previously, it advances an institutional responsibility agenda. Third, the range of institution types is considered, including community colleges, which are routinely overlooked in most of the scholarship on Black men in higher education. Fourth, new theoretical concepts that can enhance our understanding of how institutional contexts and the interactions that take place within them influence student success for Black males are offered, as are strategies for recruiting and retaining them.

On a final note, I'd like to conclude with another remark from Dr. Bensimon—one that I have personally observed her deliver with the greatest of eloquence and conviction. Ensuring that Black men have access to an equitable and transformative higher education experience is something we should do simply because it's the *right* thing to do. But in addition, we should do it because it has implications for the social and economic vitality of our country. We cannot continue to prosper as a country when a large segment of its population is relegated to a second-class education. As the old saying goes, when one of us fails, we *all* fail.

Frank Harris III
San Diego, CA, USA
April 2014

Series Editor Introduction

We are pleased to include J. Luke Wood's and Robert T. Palmer's book *Black Men in Higher Education* in our "Key Issues on Diverse College Students" series with Routledge Press. Wood and Palmer's work exemplifies the quality of research that we aim to foster within the series. It is well researched and has a practical approach.

African Americans have always placed a great value on higher education and this value is further evidenced by the 240 percent increase in the number of Blacks attending college (1984–2009). However, when the numbers are broken down by gender, Black males have not fared as well as their female counterparts in terms of enrollment and degree completion. Black males only account for 4.3 percent of the enrollment at colleges and universities in this country, and this figure has remained fairly constant for some thirty years.

With this as a backdrop, Wood and Palmer's book delves into the educational challenges facing Black male students. In addition, their book provides higher education scholars and practitioners with significant research-based, theoretical, and practical recommendations to better prepare them in assisting Black men to become more successful in higher education. Of note, Wood and Palmer highlight several models of success that can be scaled up and replicated.

Administrators, advisors, counselors, and scholars will benefit from reading Wood and Palmer's book as will the general public. It is well researched, beautifully written, and important in our quest to understand the methods, strategies, and reasons behind and for college student success of African American men.

Marybeth Gasman and Nelson Bowman III
Series Editors

Preface

Over the years, there has been much discussion about the state of Black males in education and society in general. This discussion has spawned policy reports, journals devoted to interrogating the lives and educational experiences of Black men, books, and research centers dedicated to improving educational outcomes among Black males and other men of color. Contributing to the scholarly and practical resources on Black males, President Obama has recently implemented an initiative, My Brother's Keeper, with the intent of creating opportunities of success for young men of color. This initiative will bring together foundations and companies to implement strategies that support boys and men of color in school in order to prevent their involvement in the criminal justice system.

While it is great that the topic of improving the pathway of success for Black males has garnered tremendous attention from the academic community and governmental leaders, many of the aforementioned scholarly and practical resources do not provide innovative, actionable strategies and solutions to ameliorate educational outcomes among Black males in postsecondary education. Similar to Fred Bonner's (2014a) book, *Building on Resilience: Models and Frameworks on Black Male Success across the P-20 Pipeline*, this book provides strategies and solutions that faculty, administrators, student affairs practitioners, and other institutional stakeholders could use to help improve academic success among Black men in higher education.

In addition, this book also offers another distinctive contribution to the literature on Black men in higher education. Specifically, this book provides approaches to help increase success among Black males while considering the applicability of those approaches to diverse institutional environments, such as historically Black colleges and universities, community colleges, and predominantly White institutions. Doing this is prudent because Black males have different experimental realities in each of these diverse institutions.

Many of the recommendations in this book are predicated on one of the book's primary themes, which emphasizes that while ensuring student success is a delicate balance between institution and student, in many instances, the institution can assume a more prominent role to align its programs, policies, practices, and strategies to support student success. One of the ways that they can do this is by avoiding deficit-oriented approaches that often undergirds research and the implementation of campus programs targeting Black males. Another way that institutions can do this is by providing supportive, equitable, and empowering educational climates that foster the full potential of Black males.

This book is comprised of six chapters. Chapter 1 provides the foundation for the book by contextualizing the present status of Black males in higher education as well as their experiences in diverse institutional types. In Chapter 2, we discuss the experiences of Black males in PreK-12 as well as factors internal and external to the university that help to facilitate their persistence and graduation. In Chapter 3, we provide an overview of models and theories that have been developed to examine the experiences of Black men in higher education. In particular, we highlight models that are attentive to the distinctive with-group and between-institutional realities of Black men. In Chapter 4, we propose a new model, which emphasizes the importance of context, actions, and outcomes (e.g., CAO) for studying Black males in higher education. This model underscores the critical role that institutions play in promoting success for Black males. In Chapter 5, we further contextualize this model and discuss its applicability to researching Black men in diverse institutional settings. In Chapter 6, we discuss recommendations for diverse institutions to help them recruit, support, and retain Black males.

Altogether, this book provides a comprehensive synthesis of research on Black men while also providing new directions for this line of inquiry. We have intentionally focused on addressing three themes (i.e., differential experiences across institutional type, the importance of institutional responsibility, and actionable strategies) that can serve to advance outcomes for Black men in postsecondary education.

Acknowledgments

Collectively, we would like to thank Drs. Marybeth Gasman and Nelson Bowman for allowing us to contribute this volume to their series. Thank you for allowing this book to come to fruition. We would also like to acknowledge Heather D. Jarrow from Routledge for her continuous support of work that advances equity discourse in higher education. In addition, we would like to acknowledge the scholars and practitioners who have labored arduously to advance the success of Black boys and men in education.

J. Luke Wood would like to thank God for his continual blessings and grace. He would also like to thank his wife Idara, daughter Mayen, and son Luke Jr for their love, as well as Frank Harris III for his mentorship and friendship. He would also like to acknowledge Robert T. Palmer for being an incredible colleague and thought leader.

Robert T. Palmer would like to thank J. Oscar Simmons for being supportive, kind, caring, engaging, honest, and different. He would also like to acknowledge J. Luke Wood for being an integral part of the book's process.

Chapter 1

Framing the Context

Examining the Status of Black Men in Higher Education

In recent years, there has been a proliferation of scholarship devoted to understanding the college experiences of Black men in higher education. These scholarly resources have appeared in the form of books, such as *Helping African American Men Succeed in College* (Cuyjet, 2006); *Black Men in College: Implications for HBCUs and Beyond* (Palmer & Wood, 2012); *African American Males and Education: Researching the Convergence of Race and Identity* (Dancy & Brown, 2012); *Advancing Black Male Student Success Preschool Through PhD* (Harper & Wood, 2014); and *Black Male Collegians: Increasing Access, Retention, and Persistence in Higher Education* (Palmer, Wood, Dancy, & Strayhorn, 2014). Similarly, these resources have also been manifested in the form of journals, such as *Challenge Journal: A Journal of Research on African American Men* (2007); *Journal of African American Males in Education (JAAME)* (2010); *Journal of Black Masculinity* (2010); and most recently, *Spectrum: A Journal of Black Men* (2012).

While the sheer volume of scholarly resources is noteworthy, it draws attention to the fact that educators, stakeholders, researchers, practitioners, and policymakers have raised concerns about the lack of progress that Black males have made in accessing and succeeding in postsecondary education (Bonner & Bailey, 2006; Cuyjet, 1997, 2006; Dancy, 2012; Dancy & Brown, 2012; Harper, 2006, 2012; Harper & Harris, 2012; Jackson & Moore, 2006, 2008; Palmer, Davis, & Hilton, 2009; Palmer & Wood, 2012; Strayhorn, 2008, 2010; Wood, 2012a; Wood & Turner, 2011). Social scientists have noted that Black men account for 4.3 percent of the total enrollment at four-year postsecondary institutions in the United States generally (Harper, 2006, 2012; Palmer & Strayhorn, 2008; Palmer et al., 2009; Strayhorn, 2008, 2010). Meanwhile, data from the Digest of Education Statistics (2011) has shown that that Black men account for only 5.18 percent of total postsecondary enrollment specifically. This percentage is concerning given that college-age Black men (ages 18 to 54) accounted for 6.24 percent of the population among this age bracket (U. S. Census, 2000). Incidentally, the percentage of Black men who are enrolled in college is nearly the same as it was in 1976 (Harper, 2006, 2012; Palmer et al., 2009; Palmer & Strayhorn, 2008; Strayhorn, 2008, 2010).

According to national data, two-thirds of Black men who start college will never finish (Cuyjet, 2006; Harper, 2006; Palmer et al., 2009). Interestingly, a recent version of the *Minorities in Higher Education Status* report (Kim, 2011) by the American Council on Education indicated that enrollment in higher education has increased among Black students. Nevertheless, a close examination of this report illustrates that Black females have surpassed the enrollment and success of Black males in higher education. For example, as indicated in Table 1.1, Black men accounted for 4.57 percent of the undergraduate population in 1976. More than three decades later, their representation has risen by less than one point (0.86 percent to be exact) to 5.43 percent. Compared to their female counterparts, Black men have long been underrepresented at the collegiate level. Indeed Black women have outpaced Black men in undergraduate enrollment, a trend that has continued to rise over time. While the percentage difference was only 0.87 percent in 1976, the percentage gap increased to 3.93 percent in 2010.

The dismal representation of Black men in college is even more apparent at the graduate level. For example, in 1976 Black males represented only 2.5 percent of graduate enrollment in degree-granting institutions. This percentage remained stagnant for more than two decades, with an increase to 3.61 percent in 2010. While between-gender disparities are evident at the undergraduate level,

Table 1.1 Percentage of Black Males and Females among Enrollees in Degree-Granting Institutions

	1976	1980	1990	2000	2010
Black Male Undergraduate (%)	4.57	4.09	3.74	4.38	5.43
Black Female Undergraduate (%)	5.44	5.64	5.84	7.38	9.36
% Difference	*−0.87*	*−1.55*	*−2.10*	*−3.00*	*−3.93*
Black Male Post baccalaureate (%)	2.50	2.19	1.97	2.70	3.61
Black Female Post baccalaureate (%)	3.22	3.23	3.39	5.70	8.71
% Difference	*−0.72*	*−1.04*	*−1.42*	*−3.00*	*−5.10*
Black Male Total (%)	4.27	3.83	3.50	4.14	5.18
Black Female Total (%)	5.12	5.31	5.51	7.15	9.27
% Difference	*−0.85*	*−1.48*	*−2.01*	*−3.01*	*−4.09*

Source: Digest of Education Statistics (2011).

they are even more pronounced among post baccalaureates. Though Black men accounted for 3.61 percent of the total post baccalaureate population, Black women represented 8.71 percent (a difference of 5.10 percent). These data illustrate two critical points. First, Black men are underrepresented at the collegiate level in comparison to their total proportion in the general college-age population. Second, Black women are enrolled at the undergraduate and post baccalaureate level at higher rates than their male peers; a trend that continues to persist.

In an article published in the *Economics of Education Review*, Levin, Belfield, Muennig, and Rouse (2007) indicated that increasing educational success among Black males is not only a moral issue, but also it has significant benefits to society. They argued, for example, that Black males with at least a high school diploma would have improved health status, lower rates of morality, and be in a better position to financially contribute to society. Similarly, Nevarez and Wood (2010) indicated that there are numerous benefits to a college education. For example, they noted that earning a college degree is associated with increased earning potential. While a Black male can expect to earn $30,723 a year with a high school diploma, with a bachelor's degree their mean earnings rise to $55,655. While these data reflect the significance of achieving successive levels of education, the economic benefits of a degree differ by race. For example, White men achieve higher mean earnings per year than their Black counterparts. A White male with a high school diploma will earn $5,695 more per year than a Black male with the same degree. Moreover, White men with bachelor's and master's degrees earn $15,631 ($71,286 per year) and $22,886 ($91,776 per year) more than Black men, respectively (U. S. Census Bureau, 2012). Indeed, given the under-achievement of Black men in postsecondary education, the subsequent section of this chapter will discuss theories and perspectives that attempt to provide insight into the dearth of progress among this demographic.

THEORIES AND PERSPECTIVES ON THE UNDERACHIEVEMENT OF BLACK MALES IN EDUCATION

Despite the myriad of benefits associated with receiving an education, especially a college education, Black males have made minimal advancement in postsecondary education. Some scholars have articulated theories and per-spectives to account for the stagnation among Black males in education. For example, Fordham and Ogbu (1986) introduced 'acting White,' to explain the lack of advancement among Black students in education. Specifically, Fordham and Ogbu explained that because Blacks have experienced oppression, enslavement, and discrimination in America, they have formed an oppositional culture, which acts as a bulwark between Black and White America. This

3

oppositional culture, Fordham and Ogbu posited, has provoked Blacks to persuade their same-race peers to devalue academic success because of its association with 'acting White.'

According to Lundy (2003), Blacks who subscribe to this mindset of 'acting White' view academically inclined Blacks as abandoning their Black cultural identity and rejecting their cultural norms. Some researchers have been critical of 'acting White' and its applicability to Blacks. For example, Tyson, Darity, and Castellino (2005) explained that Blacks are no less engaged in academic-related activities than their White peers. Moreover, Cook and Ludwig (1998) suggested that Blacks have a desire to attend college, spend an equal amount of time on homework, and have similar rates of absenteeism compared to their White counterparts from the same socio-economic status. Notwithstanding this criticism, some support 'acting White' in accounting for the lack of advancement in education, particularly among Black males (Fordham & Ogbu, 1986; Lundy, 2003, 2005). Specifically, Bush and Bush (2013b) have noted that Black males do not reject education, as education is viewed as a pathway for upward economic and social mobility. Instead, they argue that Black males reject schooling: the practices that are in place in education that alienate and marginalize them. In this light, 'acting White' would be viewed as a rejection of schooling, not education. This raises the importance of institutional responsibility for modifying 'schooling' practices, a theme that is addressed throughout this volume.

Other researchers have linked Black males' perception of schooling as being incongruous with their masculinity. These researchers suggest that this dissonance is another factor responsible for Black male underachievement in education (Davis, 2003; hooks, 2004; Majors & Billson, 1992). Specifically, Majors and Billson broached the concept of 'cool pose' to understand patterns of masculine expression among Black men of all ages. They posited that 'cool pose' is a strategy that Black men use to cope with oppression and social alienation. According to Harris, Palmer, and Struve (2011), Black men express 'cool pose' "through styles of speaking, gesturing, dressing, wearing hair, walking, standing, and shaking hands. The ritualized acts are directed at the dominant culture and allow Black men to express pride, strength, and control in opposition to White male masculine norms" (p. 50). Some have noted that 'cool pose' causes Black men to distance themselves from activities associated with White and feminine values, such as education (Corbin & Pruitt, 1999; Harris et al., 2011; Jackson & Moore, 2008; Palmer et al., 2009). Others have argued that 'cool pose' causes Black men to express masculinities by emphasizing sexual promiscuity, toughness, and physical expressions of power (Majors & Billson, 1992; Majors, Tyler, Peden, & Hall, 1994).

Researchers have also attributed negative images about Black males that they are exposed to in the media as a reason for their lack of advancement in education (hooks, 2004; Jackson & Moore, 2006, 2008; Wood & Hilton, 2012). According to Palmer and Maramba (2011), the media (e.g., radio, television, print media, news) rarely highlights positive accomplishments of Black men. Instead, they commonly use their public platform to perpetuate and instigate stereotypical depictions of Blacks. Consequently, Black males are victimized by these images (Bailey & Moore, 2004; Jackson & Moore, 2006, 2008; Palmer & Maramba, 2011). The media, in this sense, widely contributes to the problems that Black men experience in education.

Stereotype threat has been noted to affect the success of Black students in education. Specifically, Claude Steele (1997) and his research associates posited that stereotype threat—"the threat of being viewed through the lens of a negative stereotype, or the fear of doing something that would inadvertently confirm that stereotype" (p. 111)—was negatively linked to the academic success of Black students in higher education. To test this theory, Steele and his colleagues tested stereotype threat by conducting studies in which groups of students were exposed to a set of negative stereotypes before completing an academic task. Steele and his associates hypothesized that the performance of the group sensitive to the negative stereotype would be negatively affected. Their findings indicated a relationship between stereotype threat and task performance on an academic task.

While stereotype threat has a negative impact of the success of Black students, researchers have tested interventions that may ameliorate the effects of it (Aronson, Fried, & Good, 2002; Good, Aronson, & Inzlicht, 2003). For example, Good et al. randomly assigned 138 seventh grade students (63 percent Hispanic, 15 percent Black, and 22 percent White) to 4 groups that were mentored by college students, in order to determine whether their mentoring intervention would ameliorate the threat of gender stereotypes and reduce the gender gap in mathematics test scores within the sample. While the first group learned about the expandable nature of intelligence, the second group learned that everyone encountered difficulty when initially transitioning into seventh grade, but that things would improve. In the third group, students learned the combination of the latter two messages. These three groups were compared to the fourth, or control, group. At the end of the school year, students completed a statewide standardized test in mathematics and reading. Using a quantitative approach, Good and colleagues discerned that, in all three experimental groups, the gender gap disappeared. While not specifically focused on race, Good et al's intervention indicates that, although stereotype threat may impede academic progress among Black students, the effects can be reduced or eliminated with interventions designed to combat stereotypes.

In addition to stereotype threat, others have noted that racial discrimination plays a critical role in limiting the academic advancement of Black males (Green, 2000; Moore, 2000). For example, in the book *Brothers of the academy: Up and coming Black scholars earning our way in higher education*, Green (2000) argued that Black males are intentionally placed in inferior schools and are deprived of important resources to help maximize their educational success as a way to perpetuate social inequality. Furthermore, Hale (2001) explained that by sending Blacks to inferior schools, resulting in subpar academic preparation, White America maintains the oppression of Blacks. Hale posited that under the guise of freedom and opportunity, Blacks are blamed for their own plight. She argued, however, that racism is the culprit, preventing Blacks from achieving educational parity with their White counterparts.

In all, these theories (e.g., 'acting White,' 'cool pose,' stereotype threat) help to provide some context about the underachievement of Black males in education. While some scholars have been critical of these theories and perspectives, as illustrated in the aforementioned discussion, many researchers agree that they provide critical insight into some of the problems hindering success for Black males in education. Given that this chapter has provided some theoretical information to help contextualize the underachievement of Black males, the subsequent part of this chapter will provide further context about Black men in postsecondary education. First, this chapter will discuss enrollment of Black men by institutional control (i.e., public, private, private for-profit). Further, it will discuss the experiences and educational outcomes of Black men in diverse institutional types.

BLACK MALE ENROLLMENT IN POSTSECONDARY EDUCATION BY INSTITUTIONAL CONTROL AND TYPE

In discussing Black men in postsecondary education, it is important to acknowledge that they are enrolled in various forms of institutions, which shape and inform their experiential realities. Table 1.2 provides the percentage of undergraduate men enrolled in postsecondary education by race and institutional control. Specifically, of the total percentage of Black undergraduate men, 41.0 percent are enrolled in public two-year institutions (commonly referred to as community colleges). Given this, Bush and Bush (2010) have noted that community colleges serve as the primary pathway into postsecondary education for Black men. In contrast, only 31.2 percent are enrolled in public and private not-for-profit four-year colleges and universities (with the majority of those—23.1 percent—in public colleges).

Interestingly, a large number of Black male collegians (18.6 percent) are enrolled in private for-profit colleges and universities. This is an increased distribution, given that in 2004 only 12.0 percent of Black men were enrolled in for-profit colleges (NPSAS, 2004). This distributional percentage is larger than all groups, other than Native American/Alaskan Indian males (who enroll in for-profit colleges at 21.6 percent). This is a concerning percentage given that prior research has shown that for-profit college attendees pay higher tuition (Miller & Mupinga, 2006; Riegg, 2006), incur greater loans (Mullin, 2010), are more likely to default on their loans, and have higher levels of unemployment (United States Government Accountability Office, 2011) than public institutions. Moreover, students attending for-profit colleges tend to be less satisfied with their experiences at these institutions. For example, Wood and Vasquez Urias (2012) examined men of color who had enrolled in community colleges and proprietary schools. Six years after their enrollment, those who had attended community colleges were significantly more satisfied with their major or course of study, the quality of their education, and the cost-effectiveness of their educational pursuits.

Finally, there is another distinguishing institutional characteristic directly relevant to this discussion on Black males in higher education. While there are more than 3 million Black men enrolled in colleges and universities around the nation, more than 100,000 (101,644 to be exact) are enrolled in institutions designated as historically Black colleges and universities (HBCUs) (see Table 1.3). HBCUs are defined by federal law as colleges and universities with a mission focus on serving African Americans that were established prior to 1964 (Lee, 2012). There are a total of 105 HBCUs in the nation serving over 300,000 students; these institutions are diverse, ranging in size, have religious affiliation (e.g., religious, nonsectarian), and enrollment selectivity (Gasman, 2008; Gasman, Baez, Drezner, Sedgwick, Tudico, & Schmid, 2007). Given that most HBCUs are four-year institutions, the majority of Black males who attend HBCUs

Table 1.2 Percentage of Men by Race Enrolled in Postsecondary Education by Sector

Institutional Sector	Public four-year	Private not-for-profit four-year	Public two-year	Private for-profit	Others or more than one
Total	30.4	11.7	39.2	10.8	7.9
Black	23.1	10.1	41.0	18.6	7.3
White	32.8	13.3	37.3	8.7	7.9
Latino	25.3	7.1	46.6	12.9	8.1
Asian	38.1	12.6	34.0	6.7	8.6
American Indian or Alaska Native	26.0	6.1	36.9	21.6	9.4
Native Hawaiian/ other Pacific Islander	27.7	9.2	45.2	9.0	8.8
Other	28.8	13.9	39.9	9.9	7.5

Source: National Postsecondary Student Aid Study (NPSAS) (2012).

Table 1.3 Black Male Enrollment in HBCUs by Institutional Level and Control, Fall 2010

	Total	Public four-year	Public two-year	Private four-year	Private two-year
Total Number	101,644	65,552	7,116	28,904	72
Percent (%)	100	64.49	7.0	28.43	<1

Source: Digest of Education Statistics (2011).

are enrolled in public four-year HBCUs (64.5 percent) while 38.4 percent of Black males are enrolled in private not-for-profit HBCUs (Table 1.3).

In totality, the aforementioned data on enrollment by institutional control convey several primary points. First, the distribution of Black men by institutional control demonstrates that public two-year colleges serve as their primary avenue of access into postsecondary education. Second, a sizeable distribution of Black men is enrolled in for-profit colleges, based on data previously presented, a trend of increasing enrollment in this sector is apparent. Third, in comparison to their White and Asian male peers, Black men are more likely to be distributed in public two-year colleges and for-profit colleges, but less likely to be distributed in public and private not-for-profit four-year colleges and universities. Fourth, HBCUs serve as critical institutions that provide access to postsecondary education for Black men.

EXPERIENCES AND EDUCATIONAL OUTCOMES OF BLACK MEN IN DIVERSE INSTITUTIONAL TYPES

As illustrated by the aforementioned data, Black men are enrolled in diverse institutions in higher education. While the previous section of this chapter focused on Black male institutional enrollment, this aspect of the chapter will discuss the experiences and outcomes of Black men in diverse institutions, such as predominately White institutions (PWIs), HBCUs, and community colleges.[1]

Black Men at Predominantly White Institutions

The literature is saturated with results that indicate that Black men experience a chilly campus climate at PWIs (Allen, 1992; Cuyjet, 1997, 2006; Feagin, Vera, & Imani, 1996; Fries-Britt & Turner, 2002; Harper, Davis, Jones, McGowan, Ingram, & Platt, 2011; Strayhorn, 2008). Black men at PWIs experience alienation (Feagin et al., 1996; Fries-Britt & Turner, 2002), have unsupportive relationships with faculty (Guiffrida, 2005; Hurtado & Carter, 1997; Smedley,

Myers, & Harrell, 1993), and are likely to view the curriculum as culturally exclusive. Further evidence suggests that faculty at PWIs have low expectations and stereotypical notions about the intellectual abilities of Black men. Specifically, Bonner and Bailey (2006) explained that some faculty members perceive Black men as having poor academic socialization and low expectations for their educational success. Given these experiences, many Black men have developed a 'prove them wrong mentality,' which enables them to become even more determined to succeed when there are doubts about their ability to be successful (Moore, Madison-Colomore, & Smith, 2003). Given the experiences that Black students have with faculty, they are more inclined to seek support from Black faculty, who they view as demonstrating characteristics of othermothering (providing a familial-like source of support) (Guiffrida, 2005).

The competitive nature of the academic environment of PWIs serves as another challenge to the academic success of Black men. Bonner and Bailey (2006) posited that as Black men become socially integrated into the campus environment of PWIs, they find themselves at odds with the cutthroat competition fostered by these institutions. According to Bonner and Bailey (2006), these environments are less likely to produce the best learning outcomes for Black men, for whom social-oriented, academic climates are critical for learning and growth.

Interestingly, while research has shown that sense of belonging for Black men hinges, in part, on interacting with peers from diverse racial and ethnic backgrounds (Strayhorn, 2008), Harper and colleagues (2011) explained: "[The belongingness of Black men] is constantly threatened by the reinforcement of racist stereotypes that stigmatize them as unqualified students who gained access to the institution through affirmative action or participation on an intercollegiate sports team . . ." (p. 180). According to Harper and Kuykendall (2012), these stereotypes pose serious threats to the academic achievement of Black men at PWIs. Other scholars have provided similar accounts of these experiences for Black men at PWIs (Cuyjet, 1997, 2006; Davis, 1994; Fries-Britt & Turner, 2001; Strayhorn, 2008). Given the experiences of Black men at PWIs, these institutions must continue to improve the campus milieu so that Black students feel comfortable and supported to help facilitate their growth and development.

Black Men at HBCUs

Research has shown that Black students at HBCUs have stronger academic self-concepts, are more satisfied with their college experience, and are engaged at higher levels than their same race counterparts at PWIs (Fleming, 1984; Fries-Britt & Turner, 2002; Harper & Gasman, 2008). Other scholars have supported the impact that HBCUs have on the retention and persistence of Black students (e.g., Gasman, 2008; Gasman, Lundy-Wagner, Ransom, & Bowman, 2010; Ross,

1998). According to Kim and Conrad (2006), HBCUs are unique because they are able to positively facilitate student success despite lacking funding parity with their PWI counterparts. This is due to the culture of support that is fostered at HBCUs for Black students.

Research overwhelmingly supports the impact that HBCUs have on Black students. However, in a recent report on enrollment trends at HBCUs, Gasman (2013) suggested that a number of HBCUs have high attrition rates because they disproportionately enroll a high number of first-generation, low-income, Pell-eligible students. Furthermore, similar to other researchers (Harper & Gasman, 2008; Kimbrough & Harper, 2006; Palmer & Young, 2009), Gasman noted a gender imbalance on many HBCU campuses. Specifically, she indicated that there are five HBCUs that have more men than women enrolled; however, on the majority of HBCU campuses, the opposite is true.

While HBCUs serve as important institutions that facilitate access and success for Black students in general and Black men specifically, more Black women are enrolling in HBCUs and graduating more frequently than Black men. To this end, Kimbrough and Harper (2006) asserted that more research was needed on the experiences of Black men at these institutions. Since their observation, additional research has emerged on this demographic of students at HBCUs (Harper & Gasman, 2008; Lundy-Wagner & Gasman, 2011; Palmer & Gasman, 2008; Palmer & Strayhorn, 2008; Palmer & Wood, 2012). For example, Palmer et al. (2009) examined challenges to the retention and persistence of Black men at an HBCU and found that poor help-seeking behavior, lack of financial aid, and problems at home were salient challenges to the success of Black men.

Additional research on Black men at HBCUs has indicated that these institutions need to be more proactive and intentional about understanding the contemporary experiences of Black men on their campuses (Kimbrough & Harper, 2006; Palmer & Maramba, 2012). For example, in a study, Kimbrough and Harper (2006) found that Black men had difficulty finding caring and committed mentors and role models at HBCUs. Specifically, the participants noted that the few caring mentors and role models were sought by all the students, which created a burden on faculty and staff. In addition, participants in Kimbrough and Harper's study also noted that females got preferential treatment from the overwhelmingly male professoriate because of their physical appearance.

Similarly, in a study using Schlossberg's theory of mattering, Palmer and Maramba (2012) found that HBCUs could be more proactive in creating conditions of mattering to enhance persistence for Black men. Findings from this study indicated that faculty could be more intentional about establishing relationships with Black males outside the classroom; they could be more flexible and understanding with students; and they should go beyond lecturing in the classroom to help stimulate engagement among Black male students. Though research has demonstrated that HBCUs are very important institutions to higher education, fewer Black students are accessing these institutions as in prior years. Nevertheless, HBCUs continue to play an important role in the educational achievement of Black students. While such is the case, it is clear that more research on Black men at HBCUs is warranted.

Black Men at Community Colleges

As noted earlier, by total numbers of Black men enrolled, community colleges serve the majority of Black male students in postsecondary education. However, research on Black men in these institutions is dwarfed by that of Black men in other institutional types (Wood & Turner, 2011). It is important to recognize that there are significant differences between Black men at four-year institutions and their counterparts in community colleges (Flowers, 2006; Wood, 2013). Black men in community college are more likely to be older, married, have dependents, and to have delayed their enrollment into postsecondary education. In addition, they are also less likely to have higher degree expectations, to have graduated from private high schools, or to have enrolled in college preparation courses in foreign language, mathematics, and science (Wood, 2013). While research indicates that community colleges help to facilitate access to postsecondary opportunities for Black students (Bush & Bush, 2005; Wood, 2012a–c, 2013; Wood & Turner, 2011), a large contingent of Black men who begin their post-secondary education through community college do not persist to graduation or transfer to four-year institutions (Bush & Bush, 2005; Hagedorn, Maxwell, & Hampton, 2001–2002; Strayhorn, 2011; Wood, 2012, 2013; Wood & Hilton, 2012; Wood, Hilton, & Lewis, 2011; Wood & Turner, 2011). Black men are at an increased likelihood of prematurely departing from community college compared to men of other racial and ethnic groups (Hagedorn et al., 2001–2002; Wood, 2011; Wood & Hilton, 2012).

Esters and Mosby (2007) documented the premature departure of Black men from community colleges. Using data from the Integrated Postsecondary Education Data System (IPEDS), they found that Black men have the lowest graduation rates compared to males from other racial/ethnic groups, with only 16 percent graduating in a three-year timespan. However, one challenge in using federal data for understanding Black male success in the community college is that the calculations include only first-time, full-time certificate- and degree-seeking students. In contrast, community colleges have large non-credit student populations. Moreover, the majority of Black male community college students (60 percent) are not full-time attendees, but part-timers (Wood & Essien-Wood, 2012). Another measure of student success is achievement. Wood and Turner (2011) argued that Black males have the lowest mean grade point average of men in community colleges. Specifically, using 2006 data from the U. S. Department of Education, Wood and Turner explained that White, Latino, and Asian American males had an average GPA of 2.90, 2.75, and 2.84 respectively, whereas Black men had a GPA of 2.64.

While Black men may encounter problems in community colleges that impede their ability to graduate or transfer to a four-year institution, scholars have identified factors that are related to the success of these men in community colleges (see Mosby, 2009; Rideaux, 2004; Strayhorn, 2011, 2012; Wood, 2011, 2012, 2013; Wood & Williams, 2013). For example, Hagedorn, Maxwell, and Hampton (2001–2002) found that younger students were more likely to persist than older students. Similarly, researchers (e.g., Mason, 1994; Stevens, 2006; Wood, 2010) have identified family support as important to the success of Black men in community colleges. This research suggests that when Black men receive family support, primarily from their mothers, their chances of succeeding are increased.

Research has identified faculty interaction as salient to the success of Black community college students (Bush & Bush, 2010; Wood, 2012c). While Wood and Turner (2011) identified four factors critical to positive faculty–student interaction for Black male community students, research indicates that Black men in community college perceive faculty as unsupportive and not invested in their success (Bush & Bush, 2010; Wood, 2012). They found that faculty members must be friendly with students, illustrate authentic care, be attentive to student concerns, and proactively address academic progress. Their findings illustrate the importance of institutional affiliates in assuming responsibility for student success. Despite the fact that some research has provided context about the experiences of Black men in the community colleges, more research is needed to provide insight into the experiences of this demographic at these institutions.

EDUCATIONAL OUTCOMES AMONG BLACK MEN AT DIVERSE INSTITUTIONS

Success rates (e.g., persistence, achievement, attainment) for Black men vary greatly by institutional type. Table 1.4 presents attainment rates as a guidepost for examining cross-institutional success. The data in the table is based on the longitudinal outcomes data from the 2003–2004 beginning postsecondary students longitudinal study (BPS, 2009a). Attainment was operationalized as part-time and full-time students who achieved a certificate, associate's degree, or bachelor's degree by 2009. At public and private not-for-profit four-year colleges, slightly less than half (48.6 percent and 49.2 percent) of Black men will obtain a degree in six years. This rate is higher than that at for-profit institutions (41.3 percent). At public two-year institutions, the attainment rate is much lower at 24.0 percent. It is important to note that not all students enter the community college with the intent of earning a certificate or degree. Some students will intend to transfer (without earning a degree) while other students will have no

Table 1.4 First Degree Type Attained through 2009 by First Institution Sector (Level and Control) 2003–04 for Race/Ethnicity (Black or African American) and for Gender (Male)

First degree type attained through 2009	Attained	No degree	Total (%)
Total	35.6	64.4	100
Public four-year	48.6	51.4	100
Private not-for-profit four-year	49.2	50.8	100
Public four-year	24.0	76.0	100
Private for-profit	41.3	58.7	100
Others	22.0	78.0	100

Source: BPS (2009a).

degree intentions at all (Wood & Palmer, 2014). For instance, in these data, 11.3 percent had no degree intentions (BPS, 2009b). Regardless of these considerations, the attainment outcomes for Black men in public two-year institutions are concerning.

As noted previously, HBCUs present another layer of complexity in contextualizing the effect of institutional type on Black male success. A number of scholars has underscored the importance and success of HBCUs in fostering success for their students (Allen & Jewel, 2002; Davis, 1994; Fries-Britt & Turner, 2002; Palmer & Gasman, 2008; Palmer & Wood, 2012). Specifically, these scholars extol that HBCUs provide environments that promote belonging, affirmation, Black identity, and personal growth (Allen, 1992; Bonous-Hammarth & Boatsman, 1996; Flowers, 2002; Outcalt & Skewes-Cox, 2002). The tangible outcomes of such environments are evident in viewing data for the total degrees awarded to Black men. While HBCUs account for only 2.1 percent of the 4,868 degree-granting institutions, they do a good job at graduating Black men (especially at the bachelor's and doctoral levels) (see Table 1.5). However, as noted, Black women have higher graduation rates than men at these institutions (see Table 1.6). For example, while HBCUs awarded 9,327 bachelor's degrees to Black men in 2009–2010, they awarded 17,570 bachelor's degrees to Black women during this time frame. Similarly, at the doctoral level, HBCUs awarded 454 doctoral degrees to Black men while Black women were awarded 826 doctoral degrees in 2009–2010 (Digest of Education Statistics, 2011).

Based upon the aforementioned data, some institutional types perform better in fostering Black male attainment than others, particularly private not-for-profit and public four-year institutions. While this is encouraging news, it is interesting

13

Table 1.5 Total Degrees Awarded to Black Men by HBCU and All Institutions in 2009–2010

Degree type	HBCU total	All institutions total	HBCU percent of all institutions
Associate's	516	36,136	1.42
Bachelor's	9,327	56,171	16.60
Master's	1,488	22,120	6.72
Doctoral	454	3,622	12.53

Source: Digest of Education Statistics (2011).

Table 1.6 Total Degrees Awarded to Black Females by HBCU and All Institutions in 2009–2010

Degree type	HBCU total	All institutions total	HBCU percent of all institutions
Associate's	1,155	77,769	1.49
Bachelor's	17,570	108,673	16.17
Master's	4,075	54,338	7.50
Doctoral	826	6,795	12.16

Source: Digest of Education Statistics (2011).

when considering the campus climate for Black men at these institutions. This suggests a greater need to focus on programming and interventions at these colleges that can increase their capacity to serve Black men. As indicated, while HBCUs serve as a critical linchpin in fostering the success of Black men, Black women outperform their male counterparts in terms of access and graduation rates. Nevertheless, as noted, these institutions award a significantly high proportion of degrees to Black men, especially at the bachelor and doctoral degree levels. Given the data highlighted in this chapter, it is clear that this book on ensuring success among Black men is timely, relevant, and necessary.

CONCLUDING REMARKS

Although research has shown that Black students are making progress in terms of accessing and succeeding in higher education, the number of Black men entering postsecondary education has been stagnant. In fact, researchers note that the enrollment of Black men in higher education comprises 4.3 percent, which is the same percentage enrolled in 1976. This chapter has discussed some theories (e.g., 'acting White,' 'cool pose,' stereotype threat) that attempt to provide an understanding of the underrepresentation of Black men in education. Furthermore, this chapter has highlighted the importance of institutional responsibility for student outcomes by discussing the enrollment and educational experiences of Black men in diverse institutions. While Chapter 2 will discuss critical challenges in PreK-12 that pose barriers to the success of Black men as they transition to higher education, this chapter has provided a critical foundation for this book by contextualizing the underrepresentation of Black men in postsecondary education in general and discussing their enrollment and experiences in diverse institutions specifically.

NOTE

1   Although this chapter has provided an overview on the enrollment of Black men in for-profit institutions, given that there is a scarcity of literature that highlights their experiences within those contexts, this chapter is unable to provide further information about Black men in for-profit institutions.

Chapter 2

Factors Affecting the Success of Black Males in PreK-12 and Higher Education

In Chapter 1, we provided an overview of the current status of Black men in higher education. We juxtaposed this with historical information about the enrollment of Black men in postsecondary education. Furthermore, in addition to discussing some theoretical underpinnings and perspectives researchers have cited for the stagnation among Black men in higher education, Chapter 1 also discussed their enrollment, experiences, and educational outcomes in diverse postsecondary institutions. The focus of this current chapter is to review literature on Black male collegians. Specifically, this review will encompass the following: (a) funding disparities between low-income and affluent school districts; (b) academic tracking; (c) underrepresentation in gifted education program and advanced placement courses; (d) unqualified teachers; and (e) low expectations among teachers and counselors regarding the academic potential of Black males as well as their high rates of suspension/expulsion in PreK-12 schools. A critical component of this review will be to examine factors that help to facilitate student engagement for Black men in postsecondary education. We are particularly attentive to factors that promote student engagement within the context of diverse institutions.

THE PRECOLLEGE EXPERIENCE OF BLACK MALES

Research has shown that academic problems hindering the educational progress of Black males begin early, impinging on their ability to complete high school (Davis, 2003; Epps, 1995; Garibaldi, 2007; Howard-Hamilton, 1997). A strong body of literature has indicated that a student's academic preparation prior to college is significantly related to their ability to access and succeed in higher education (Cuyjet, 1997, 2006; Davis, 2003; Garibaldi, 2007; Harper, 2006, 2012; Jackson & Moore, 2006, 2008; Strayhorn, 2008). Despite this, Black males are less likely to receive a quality education in PreK-12, causing potential impediments to their accessibility and success in college.

Black males are less likely to attend schools that are funded to the same degree as schools attended by their White counterparts. In many cases, schools are funded through local property taxes. Thus, schools in more affluent neighborhoods receive more funding per pupil than schools in less wealthy communities. This puts many Black students at a disadvantage because they are more likely to live in inner cities and under-resourced communities (Nevarez & Wood, 2007). For example, data from the National Assessment of Educational Progress (NAEP) show that, while 3 percent of White eighth graders are in schools where more than 75 percent of the students qualify for free or reduced lunch, 35 percent of eighth grade Blacks are in such schools (Flores, 2007). Due to this funding system and the fact that many Black students are more likely to come from less affluent communities, school districts that serve a large number of Black students receive less local and state funding to educate students, compared with school districts that serve a low percentage of minority students (Garibaldi, 2007; Jackson & Moore, 2006, 2008; Palmer et al., 2009; Strayhorn, 2008).

The funding disparity between school districts is tightly coupled with the kind of resources their schools are able to provide for students. For example, schools with more resources are able to offer smaller classes, which positively contribute to student learning and achievement (Garibaldi, 2007; Jackson & Moore, 2006, 2008). This puts Black students at a disadvantage, given that they disproportionately attend schools with fewer resources and, therefore, larger class sizes. Moreover, because Black students attend PreK-12 schools that receive less funding, these schools typically are less able to provide the latest books, laboratories, instructional material, and technology compared to those that receive more funding (Garibaldi, 2007; Jackson & Moore, 2006, 2008).

Academic Tracking

Another factor that contributes to the disproportionate underpreparedness of Black males in higher education is academic tracking. Academic tracking is the schools' systematic placement of students in classes based upon their performance on standardized testing or teachers' perception of their academic ability (Oakes, Gamoran, & Page, 1992). Academic tracking promotes inequality because students who are placed in high-achieving academic tracks are exposed to more complex and challenging classroom instruction than those who are placed in low-achieving academic tracks. Gamoran, Porter, Smithson, and White (1997) conducted a quantitative study, using data from school districts in San Francisco and San Diego, California, and Rochester and Buffalo, New York. Using a three-level hierarchical model, they found that students in high-achieving academic tracks learned more than students in low-achieving academic tracks. Moreover, existing empirical research shows that Black males are overrepresented in low-ability or remedial tracks (Cuyjet, 1997, 2006; Garibaldi, 2007; Harper, 2006,

2012; Jackson & Moore, 2006, 2008; Palmer et al., 2009; Strayhorn, 2008; *Yes We Can, the Schott Foundation*, 2010), even when their scores on standardized assessments are equal to or better than their White peers' (Garibaldi, 2007; Jackson & Moore, 2006, 2008).

Not only are more Black males likely to be placed on lower academic tracks, they are more likely to be found in special education (Garibaldi, 2007; Moore et al., 2008; Jackson & Moore, 2006, 2008; Palmer et al., 2009; Strayhorn, 2008). According to data from recent studies, such as *Yes We Can, the Schott Foundation's 50 State Report on Public Education and Black Males*, Black and Hispanic males constitute almost 80 percent of youth in special education programs. In particular, Black boys are more likely to be represented among children classified with learning disabilities, mental impairments, and emotional–behavioral disorders (U. S. Commission on Civil Rights, 2009). Given the overrepresentation of Black males in special education, Moore et al. (2008) noted that for many school systems, placing Black males in special education seems to be the preferred educational intervention or curriculum.

Underrepresentation in Gifted Education and AP Courses

While Black males are overrepresented in remedial courses, they are under-represented in gifted education programs as well as advanced placement (AP) courses (Bonner, 2010; Garibaldi, 2007; Jackson & Moore, 2006, 2008; Ford, Moore, & Milner, 2005). Data from the *Journal of Blacks in Higher Education* (JBHE, 2008) noted that though there has been some progress in the number of Black students enrolled in AP courses, Blacks continue to lag far behind White students. For example, JBHE indicated that in 1985 there were only 2,768 Black students taking AP courses. By 1990, however, the number of Black students participating in AP programs doubled. The number of Black students taking AP courses has continued to increase over the years. In fact, in 2007, there were 51,423 Black students enrolled in AP courses. Research indicates that participating in gifted education and AP courses is important because these programs and courses have a positive impact on a variety of achievement outcomes, such as higher scores on standardized college entrance assessments, and is tied to more completed years of education (Jackson & Moore, 2006, 2008). Thus, the underrepresentation of Black males in gifted educational programs and AP courses negatively influences their preparation and subsequent success (Jackson & Moore, 2006, 2008).

In addition to providing an overview of the enrollment of Black students in AP courses, the JBHE (2008) delineated several barriers that hinder Black students from participating in AP programs. Specifically, the JBHE noted that most AP programs are concentrated in more affluent, predominantly White schools. Second, in racially integrated schools, Black students are less inclined to enroll in AP courses because they have not been adequately prepared to handle

19

the academic demands of such courses. Contributing greatly to the under-representation of Black students in gifted education or AP courses is the perception among teachers, counselors, and school administrators that Black students are intellectually inferior and not capable of coping with the rigorous curriculum of AP programs. JBHE points out that in some schools, Black students may not pursue an AP curriculum because they may face anti-intellectual pressure from their peers who may feel they are 'sell outs' or 'acting White' (see Chapter 1).

In addition to these factors, another less talked about factor that may prevent or limit the participation of Black students in AP courses is the fee associated with taking an AP exam in order to receive credit for college. According to JBHE (2008), students hoping to gain significant college credits may have to pay more than $400 to take the appropriate AP tests. Although the College Board offers a small reduction for low-income students, significantly reducing the cost of AP exams may encourage more Black students in general and Black males specifically to enroll in AP programs.

Unqualified Teachers

The underrepresentation of qualified teachers among educators who serve large numbers of Black students is another contributor to their lack of preparedness for success in higher education. Data from the Education Trust (2009) showed that core academic classes in high-poverty schools are more likely to be taught by an out-of-field teacher compared to low-poverty schools. Similarly, Flores (2007) and others (e.g., Darling-Hammond, 2000; Garibaldi, 2007; Ladson-Billings, 1997; Tate, 2008) have explained that students attending predominantly Black and Hispanic schools are twice as likely to be taught by teachers with three years of teaching experience, or less, compared to those attending predominantly White schools. Since Black students are more likely to attend these schools compared to their White counterparts, they are being handicapped to succeed in comparison to their White peers as they continue their educational trajectory in PreK-12 and beyond.

While the overexposure to unqualified teachers is a racial issue, it is also a socio-economic one. According to Mayer, Mullens, and Moore (2000), the percentage of teachers in high-poverty schools who are inexperienced is 20 percent, compared to 11 percent of those at low-poverty schools. In addition, Flores (2007) noted that, whereas out-of-field teachers teach 19 percent of classes in low-poverty schools, that figure is 34 percent in high-poverty schools. Flores also explains that the least prepared teachers are disproportionately found in under-resourced schools that are populated by low-income minority students from inner cities and rural communities. Because a disproportionate number of Black students are deprived of access to qualified teachers, which hinders achievement, efforts to ensure that they have access and are instructed by qualified teachers is a civil rights issue (Schoenfeld, 2002).

Low Expectations and High Rates of Suspensions among Black Males

In addition to unqualified teachers, researchers have also discussed that teachers' low expectations can hinder the achievement of Black males (Davis, 2003; Garibaldi, 2007; Palmer et al., 2009; Strayhorn, 2008). Specifically, research has shown that in elementary and secondary education, teachers and counselors are far more likely to impose negative expectations upon Black males as it relates to attending college than upon their White counterparts (Palmer et al., 2009). The relationship between teacher expectations and academic achievement appears to be a reciprocal one. That is, while teacher expectations influence academic achievement, students' academic performance can also affect teachers' expectations of those pupils. Teachers may be more likely to develop expectations about and treat their students in a manner that is more consistent with those students' performance on standardized assessments than their actual abilities (Thompson, Warren, & Carter, 2004). Thus, given that Black students are likely to perform lower on standardized examinations than their majority counterparts, teachers are more likely to have higher expectations for White students than students of color. In turn, research demonstrates that teacher expectations can influence academic performance, suggesting that those expectations can become a self-fulfilling prophecy for students. Moreover, such expectations can manifest into messages, which can lead to differences in teaching behavior and subsequent achievement (Jackson & Moore, 2006, 2008).

In addition to educators having low expectations for the academic success of Black males, Black males in PreK-12 are also disproportionately disciplined, more apt to face expulsions, and suspended longer and more frequently than are White students (Garibaldi, 2007; Hale, 2001; Jackson & Moore, 2006, 2008; Majors & Billson, 1992). Garibaldi noted that in the majority of the 16,000 school districts across the country, Black males had the highest rates of suspensions, expulsions, and non-promotions, and the lowest rates of secondary school graduation. More recent data from the U. S. Department of Education, gathered through the 2009–2010 Civil Rights Data Collection, echoed Garibaldi's research about the disproportionate number of suspensions among Black males. More specifically, statistics from 72,000 schools in 7,000 districts, serving approximately 85 percent of the nation's students, indicated that although Black students comprised 18 percent of those enrolled in the schools sampled, they accounted for 35 percent of those suspended once, 46 percent of those suspended more than once, and 39 percent of all expulsions. Moreover, data collected for this initiative revealed that one in five Black males and more than one in ten Black females received an out-of-school suspension.

INTERNAL FACTORS FACILITATING SUCCESS FOR BLACK MEN IN HIGHER EDUCATION

Given that the aforementioned section of this chapter has provided an insight into many of the issues that pose barriers to the success of Black males as they transition into postsecondary education, the subsequent section of this chapter will discuss internal and external factors relative to the college campus that help to facilitate Black male success. The specific factors to be discussed include: (a) student organizations; (b) faculty–student interaction; (c) peer interaction; (d) Black Male Initiatives (BMIs); and (e) mentors.

Student Organizations

Research has noted a relationship between involvement in student organizations and satisfaction with the institution for Black students (Cuyjet, 1997, 2006; Harper & Quaye, 2007; Palmer & Wood, 2012; Patton, 2006; Strayhorn, 2012). For example, in an interview with 24 students, 12 of whom who were Black, Museus (2008) found that ethnic organizations served as spaces for cultural familiarity, cultural expression and advocacy, and cultural validation for minority students at PWIs. Similarly, Patton (2006) indicated that cultural centers not only provide a 'home away from home' for Black students, they also serve as a space where they can engage in educational, purposeful activities. These organizations also offer Black men critical opportunities to establish supportive and nurturing relationships with minority faculty, staff, and students.

Furthermore, Harper and Quaye (2007) found that predominantly Black and mainstream organizations provide Black men with opportunities to become engaged in social justice-related activities. Brown (2006) explained that intramural athletics and recreational activities, student unions, and mentoring that encouraged co-curricular involvement are critical spaces that help to engender opportunities for Black male campus engagement. Brown's findings are complementary to Cuyjet's (1997) work on Black men. Cuyjet noted that given that many Black men are more inclined to participate in athletics and recreational activities, postsecondary institutions should use these venues to help increase social interactions among Black men, which might expand opportunities for them to help support each other.

Despite the many benefits students derived from being engaged on campus, Black men are generally disengaged on the campuses of PWIs and HBCUs. Given this, Palmer and Young (2009) suggested that universities should consider surveying Black men to understand what their interests are and implement activities that will increase their engagement on campus. In particular, high impact practices should be employed to engage Black men in the social milieu of campus. Co-curricular programming that is academic and career-oriented in nature should be prioritized over purely social events (Harper & Kuykendall, 2012).

Faculty–Student Interaction

Aside from student organizations, faculty–student interaction helps to facilitate student engagement. Research has shown a relationship between faculty interaction and multiple educational gains, such as academic skill development, leadership ability, occupational values, and gains in educational aspirations (Sax, Bryant, & Harper, 2005). The more interactions students have with faculty inside and outside the classroom, the greater their gains will be with student development and institutional satisfaction (Astin, 1993). Tinto (1993) argued that the more students are engaged in the institution, the more likely that they will experience opportunities to develop critical connections with faculty, which will increase their sense of belonging on campus.

Though faculty interaction is important, satisfaction with faculty relationships vary by race (Lundberg & Schreiner, 2004). For example, while White students have the greatest satisfaction with faculty relationships, the opposite is true for Black students (Davis, 1994; Feagin et al., 1996; Fleming, 1984; Fries-Britt & Turner, 2002; Guiffrida, 2005). Although recent research has shown that Black men experience unique challenges with faculty at HBCUs (e.g., Kimbrough & Harper, 2006; Palmer & Maramba, 2012), literature indicates that Black men have supportive relationships with HBCU faculty (Fleming 1984; Fries-Britt & Turner, 2002; Palmer & Gasman, 2008; Palmer & Wood, 2012). Similar to their counterparts in PWIs, Black men in community colleges perceive faculty to be unsupportive and not well invested in their success (Bush & Bush, 2010; Wood, 2014).

Promoting faculty–student engagement is a core responsibility of colleges and universities. Research from Wood and Ireland (2014) found that, despite numerous background and environment considerations, the most integral predictors of faculty–student engagement with Black males were campus services. In particular, they found that Black men who participated in orientation, study skills courses, and learning communities were more likely to experience engagement with faculty. Thus, there remains a need to ensure that effective programming is in place, which fosters climates that prepare students and faculty to engage with one another.

Peer Interaction

Peer interaction influences student engagement (Astin, 1993; Bonner & Bailey, 2006; Tinto, 1993). By interacting with peers, students have greater exposure to campus resources, student organizations, and develop a social network that can

23

be central in helping them navigate academic and non-academic dilemmas (Astin, 1993; Bonner & Bailey, 2006; Tinto, 1993). For Black students at PWIs, peers play a critical role because they help to facilitate a sense of belonging in an institutional environment that differs significantly from their cultural and socio-economic backgrounds (Bonner & Bailey, 2006).

According to Astin (1993), peer interaction facilitates academic development, problem solving skills, critical thinking, and cultural awareness for Black men. Moreover, in a study of 32 high-achieving Black male college students, Harper (2006) reported that participants' same-race peers helped to support, encourage, and validate their academic success. Palmer and Gasman (2008) found that relationships with like-minded peers, who were focused on succeeding academically, had a positive impact on the success of 11 Black men at an HBCU.

Strayhorn (2008) found that cross-racial peer interactions facilitated the sense of belonging for Black males at PWIs. Specifically, he indicated that interactions with a person of a diverse background can lead to meaningful interactions that foster a greater sense of belonging to the campus. Despite indicating that cross-racial peer interactions were significant to the sense of belonging for Black and White students, Strayhorn noted that this topic warranted additional investigation. Interestingly, according to research from Palmer et al. (2011), because students want to be prepared to compete in today's global economy, they want to have more meaningful exchanges with diverse peers. However, in a study where he and his colleagues interviewed minority students at a PWI, the students explained that institutions do little to promote cross-race interactions.

While a strong body of literature has provided some context about the outcomes associated with peer interactions for Black men at PWIs and HBCUs, little research has discussed ways in which peer interaction is linked to success for Black men in community colleges. For example, Poole (2006) identified peer support as critical to the success of Black men in community colleges, indicating that these relationships help to improve their academic and social integration. In addition, Bush and Bush (2010) indicated that peer interaction plays a vital role in determining grade point averages, transfer, and degree/certificate attainment for Black men in community colleges. However, Bush and Bush also found that peer support from other Black men was viewed as a challenge to overcome as opposed to a linchpin for success. Thus, differential effects of peer interactions may be evident across institutional types.

Black Male Initiatives

Black Male Initiatives have also been linked to Black male campus engagement (Bonner & Bailey, 2006; Bledsoe & Rome, 2006; Harper & Harris, 2012; Palmer et al., 2013; Wood & Palmer, 2012). Research has shown that BMIs function to foster academic and social integration, student engagement, sense of belonging, and create a welcoming and affirming campus environment for Black men. BMIs provide a safe place for Black men to discuss a range of issues and are critical in helping increase their success (Bonner & Bailey, 2006; Bledsoe & Rome, 2006; Palmer et al., 2013; Wood & Palmer, 2012). While evidence indicates that community colleges have BMIs to help facilitate the success of Black men (Wood, 2011; Wood & Harris, 2013), there is little research (e.g., Nevarez & Wood, 2010) to examine the efficacy of these programs. Moreover, Harper (2014) notes that the manner in which Black male initiatives are enacted on college campuses can serve to detract, rather than propel, student success. Specifically, he points to the enactment of one-day conferences as a weak intervention strategy for Black male success. In response to the weak design of many Black male initiatives, Harper and Kuykendall (2012) articulated a series of key characteristics of Black male initiatives. These are discussed in Chapter 3.

Mentors

In addition to Black male initiatives, mentors are critical to the success of Black male college students. Mentors on campus can act as critical agents that help to facilitate campus engagement for Black males (Cuyjet, 1997, 2006; Harper, 2012; LaVant, Anderson, & Tiggs, 1997; Strayhorn, 2008; Sutton, 2006). For example, Scott (2012) noted that mentors can be responsible for: (a) acclimating students to the campus environment; (b) informing students about campus involvement (e.g., clubs, organizations, activities) and professional opportunities (e.g., internship); and (c) serving as guides as students continue through college. At HBCUs, faculty members often take on the role of mentors for Black men (Fries-Britt & Turner, 2002; Gasman, 2008; Palmer & Gasman, 2008). Professors at HBCUs are often noted for going above their responsibilities to help support the success and development of Black students. While on-campus mentors are vital to the success of Black males, mentors and role models off campus also provide a critical source of support for their success (Cuyjet, 1997, 2006; Palmer & Gasman, 2008; Wood & Palmer, 2012). In addition, we contend that many initiatives designed to support Black men also rely upon intervention models that use mentoring as a strategy. However, these mentor matches fail because they do not adequately match, track, and assess the intervention. Moreover, the program design itself does not provide purposeful academic and career-oriented activities for mentor–protégé engagement.

EXTERNAL FACTORS CRITICAL TO BLACK MEN'S SUCCESS IN HIGHER EDUCATION

The previous section discussed internal factors relative to college campuses that facilitate success among Black males. This section will delineate external factors associated with academic success for Black men in higher education. They include: (a) non-cognitive factors; (b) racial and masculine identity; (c) family support; (d) spirituality; and (e) financial support.

Non-Cognitive Factors

Non-cognitive factors are strongly linked to the success of Black men in higher education (Cokley, 2003; Moore et al., 2003; Swail, Redd, & Perna, 2003; Wood & Harris, 2013). Tracey and Sedlacek (1987) identified eight non-cognitive factors critical to the success of Black students at PWIs. These factors ranged from positive self-concept to successful leadership experience. Scholars have noted strong study habits, time management skills, and the student's willingness to use services on campus as salient contributors to the success of Black students (Hrabowski, Maton, & Greif, 1998). In fact, Moore (2001) argued, "success in college has less to do with aptitude in cognitive measures . . . than non-cognitive measures such as self-efficacy, motivation, commitment, and persistence" (p. 77). Strayhorn (2013) actualized Moore's quote by underscoring the role that 'grit' (i.e., persistence, determination, and motivation) played in the success of 140 Black male students at a PWI. While research has emphasized the relationship between non-cognitive factors and success for Black men, Palmer and Strayhorn (2008) explained that institutions still have a responsibility to provide the resources to help students achieve success.

Racial and Masculine Identity

Racial identity is another non-cognitive factor researchers have attributed to the success of Black men in postsecondary education (Cokley, 2001; Hrabowski et al., 1998; Lott, 2011; Okech & Harrington, 2002). Black racial identity is rooted in William E. Cross's model of nigrescence (i.e., the process of becoming Black). Cross's model consists of several stages, which delineate how Blacks move from a White frame of reference to a positive Black frame of reference (Lott, 2011). His model includes the following phases: (a) Pre-encounter; (b) Encounter (c) Immersion–Emersion; and (d) Internalization. The initial stage (i.e., Pre-encounter) indicates that Blacks generally engage in a process of self-loathing while simultaneously valuing White values and ways. As the stages progress, Blacks internalize a more positive racial identity and learn to embrace elements of biculturalism and multiculturalism (Lott, 2011).

Nasim, Roberts, Hamell, and Young (2005) conducted a longitudinal study with 250 Black students attending a PWI and an HBCU in order to investigate the relationship between positive racial identity and academic success. Findings from their study indicated a relationship between a positive racial identity and performing well in school. In his study of 190 Black men enrolled across five research universities, Reid (2013) found similar results to Nasim et al. More specifically, he found that Black men with high grade point averages (GPA) were not only academically and socially integrated into college, but also held positive racial identity beliefs. While research supports a linkage between positive racial identity and academic success, Campbell and Fleming (2000) found the inverse for Black male students with weak racial identity. In a study of 141 Black males attending a largely minority urban university, they discovered that Black males who feared success had a weak or conflicted racial identity. The authors defined fear of success as "feelings of anxiety which arise as an individual approaches the accomplishment of important, self-defined goals, the attainment of which is both deeply desired and resisted by the individual" (p. 5).

While most research (e.g., Campbell & Fleming, 2000; Hrabowski et al., 1998; Reid, 2013) has shown a relationship between positive racial identity and academic success, some research has demonstrated a link between racial identity and sense of belonging for Black students at PWIs. Specifically, research has suggested that Black students with a positive racial identity are more likely to feel connected to the institution (Mitchell & Dell, 1992; Taylor & Howard-Hamilton, 1995). For example, Parker and Flowers (2003) administered the Racial Identity Attitude Scale to 118 Black students (59 percent male and 41 percent female) to assess the effects of racial identity on their GPA and sense of belonging. While they did not find a relationship between racial identity and GPA, they found a relationship between racial identity and sense of belonging on campus.

In addition to racial identity, more recent scholarship has explored the effect of masculine identity on collegiate success (Harris & Harper, 2008). For example, Harris and Wood (in press) contend that four distinctive masculine domains have an integral influence on male-of-color success in postsecondary education, which include: breadwinner orientation, help-seeking behaviors, school as a feminine domain, and competitive ethos. Breadwinner orientation refers to men's perceptions that providing for their families is solely a responsibility for men. Healthy perceptions of breadwinning would allow for a more balanced view that breadwinning is a role that both men and women can assume. Help-seeking behavior involves men's perceptions about whether or not they should seek out help (i.e., from campus faculty, staff, other students). Healthy conceptions of help-seeking would not perceive seeking help as making one less masculine or weak. School as a feminine domain refers to men's perceptions of school as a domain for both genders. Men with healthy perceptions of this notion would perceive that school is not solely a feminine domain, but one suitable for men as well. Finally, competitive ethos refers to men's perception of competition with other men. Preferably, men would not devalue themselves or see themselves as 'lesser than' when unable to be as competitive as they would like with other men in academic spheres.

Family Support

In addition to non-cognitive factors, research has identified family as critical to the success of Black male college students. While Tinto (1993) urged high school students transitioning into college to divorce themselves from their past communities, researchers have explained that, for minority students, family plays a vital role in their success (Guiffrida, 2004; Hurtado, Carter, & Spuler, 1996; Nora & Cabrera, 1996; Rosas & Hamrick, 2002). For example, in a study of 50 Black students, Barnett (2004) found that participants' families played an integral role in their success by decreasing stress and serving as an emotional outlet. Moreover, Palmer, Davis, and Maramba (2011) delineated that family support was instrumental to the success of 11 Black men at an HBCU. Specifically, Palmer and colleagues emphasized that although some of the participants' family members lacked formal education, they provided inspirational and encouraging messages that had a significant impact on the participants' success.

Despite the fact that evidence illustrates ways families can be supportive of the success of minorities, Guiffrida (2004) explained that families can be assets or liabilities to the success of Black students. For example, in a study of 99 Black students, which consisted of 15 students who left the university prematurely (leavers), 65 academically low-achieving students (low achievers), and 19 high-achieving students (high achievers), Guiffrida found that while the high achievers received emotional and academic support from their families, the leavers felt that their families contributed to their emotional stress, which engendered poor academic performance. Furthermore, Guiffrida noted that while the high achievers received financial support from their families, leavers wished their families would have helped them, and in some cases, felt guilty for taking money from their struggling families. Similarly, Palmer and colleagues (2009) found that although they may be attending college far from their families, events occurring in the household could possibly interfere with the academic success of Black males in college.

While most research has illustrated a relationship between family support and academic success for Black men, Strayhorn (2011) found that if Black male community college students are overwhelmed with family responsibilities, this could hinder their success. Wood (2011) found that family responsibilities were more likely to hinder the success of Black men who had recently enrolled in community college compared with those who were advancing toward graduation. This finding might indicate that Black male community college students who have progressed toward completing their degrees have learned to manage family stress compared to their counterparts who recently re-enrolled in community college.

Spirituality

Spirituality is another factor critical to the success of Black men in higher education. According to Mattis (2000), spirituality includes a belief in having a personal relationship with God and living according to God's will. Love and Talbot (1999) proposed an alternative definition, explaining that spirituality involves the pursuit of discovering meaning and purpose in one's life. Research has suggested a relationship between spirituality and retention for Black men in higher education (Herndon, 2003; Watson, 2006). In a study Herndon (2003) conducted with 13 Black male students, he found that spirituality was vital to their success. Wood and Hilton (2012) have reported similar findings for Black men in community colleges. They found that spirituality served as a core mechanism for academic success for Black men. In their study of 28 men, many men defined spirituality in a Christian religious connotation, referring to their relationship with God. They found that God/spirituality: (a) provided men with a confidant when faced with challenges; (b) served as inspiration to pursue academic excellence; (c) provided them with a clear purpose and direction in life; (d) enabled them to overcome barriers by serving as a resilience factor; and (e) reduced time committed to relational distractions (e.g., partying, womanizing). Interestingly, when investigating the link between spirituality and success for Black students at HBCUs and PWIs, Weddle-West, Hagan, and Norwood (2013) found that Black men at HBCUs scored significantly lower on the spiritual belief variable than their counterparts at PWIs. Given the challenges that Black students face at PWIs, Weddle-West and colleagues posited that Black students at PWIs may need to rely more on spirituality as a coping mechanism than HBCU students.

Financial Support

One of the most important predictors of whether minority students will leave college is the ability to finance their education (Perna, 2006; St. John, 2002; St. John & Starkey, 1995; Titus, 2006; Wood et al., 2011). According to research, concerns about financing college play a critical role in where students decide to attend college (St. John, 2002; Swail et al., 2003). For example, many Black males enroll in community colleges (National Center for Public Policy and Higher Education, 2011) and public HBCUs because they are seen as low cost options (Palmer et al., 2009). While the availability of financial support is critical to the success of Black college students, gifts in the form of scholarships and grants are paramount to the degree attainment for Black males (St. John, 2002).

Loans seem to be both positively and negatively correlated with student success. Research illustrates that loans appear to promote success among White students more than minorities (Perna & Jones, 2013). This might be due to the

29

fact that Black students are more sensitive to college costs and more averse to taking out loans to support their college education (Kaltenbaugh, St. John, & Starkey, 1999). This is particularly concerning, given that policymakers have increasingly relied on loans in the composition of financial aid packages (St. John, 2003; Wei & Carroll, 2004). Moreover, even when Black males rely on loans to finance their education, when policymakers make changes to the requirements to receive loans, some students have been less likely to be awarded loans. For example, the recent modifications to the requirements for the Parent PLUS loan (PPL) have caused many low-income students to be denied the PPL, which has severely affected student enrollment and persistence at HBCUs (Nelson, 2012).

There is evidence that employment influences success for college students, but that impact depends on the location and nature of work. Extant research suggests that working off campus is negatively associated with success (Pascarella, Edison, Nora, Hagedorn, & Terenzini, 1998). Conversely, existing empirical evidence appears to suggest that working on campus can positively influence success (Kuh, Kinzie, Buckley, Bridges, & Hayek, 2007). This being the case, the inability to pay for college, insufficient financial resources, or the need to financially support their family back home may force many Black males to work a substantial number of hours while attempting to attend college full time, thereby adversely affecting their likelihood of success (e.g., Branch-Brioso, 2009).

Evidence indicates that nearly 84 percent of community college students hold some form of employment during college (Wood et al., 2011). Moreover, Black men are often concentrated in jobs that are temporary, physically demanding, and have late night shifts (Wood & Jones, in press). Due to the need to work, many Black male students are more attracted to for-profit institutions than the traditional institutions of higher education because they offer greater flexibility to take classes (Rooks, 2013). Given this, in 2004 to 2010 Black enrollment in for-profit bachelor degree programs grew by 218 percent compared to a modest increase of 24 percent at public four-year colleges and universities (Rooks, 2013). In sum, the ability to pay for college is a critical factor influencing the success of college students. Rising college costs and increased reliance on loans all contribute to financial pressures for Black students. Given this, many Black males feel the need work to compensate for inadequate finances; working too many hours can hinder their success.

CONCLUDING REMARKS

This chapter has discussed some of the critical barriers in PreK-12 that pose significant obstacles for Black males as they access, transition into, and work toward success in higher education. Given the literature reviewed, it is clear that more research and practical engagement is needed to ensure that Black males are sufficiently prepared to succeed in postsecondary education. Similarly, this chapter has discussed internal and external factors relative to higher education that helps facilitate success for Black men. Specifically, this chapter has identified the importance of the institution (via faculty–student interactions and Black male initiatives) in supporting Black male success in diverse postsecondary education contexts.

Chapter 3

Theoretical Frameworks for Examining Black Men in College

For years, scholars and practitioners alike have examined factors that influence outcomes for males of color (particularly Black males) in education (Allen, 1986; Cuyjet, 2006; Harper, Carini, Bridges, & Hayek, 2004; Palmer & Davis, 2012; Palmer et al., 2011). Through the predominant disciplinary lenses of sociology, psychology, and human ecology, as well as interdisciplinary lenses of masculinity and Africology, the experiences of Black men have been investigated in PreK-20 educational sites. This community of inquirers has produced a variety of scholarly tools (e.g., models, frameworks) that can be used for understanding the specific educational realities of Black boys and men.

The focus of this chapter is on describing these scholarly tools. Moreover, in the subsequent section we will present an additional model that also can be used as a theoretical framework. This chapter will adhere to the following structure: (a) describing the function of theoretical frameworks; (b) articulating the inadequate use of frameworks in prior inquiry on Black men; and (c) presenting five models from the extant literature on Black men that have been either used or designed in educational research. These theoretical frameworks include: *African American Male Theory* (Bush & Bush, 2013a), the *Socio-Ecological Outcomes (SEO) model* (Harris & Wood, in press), *Expressions of Spirituality* (Herndon, 2003), *Prove-Them-Wrong Syndrome* (Moore et al., 2003), and *Capital Identity Projection* (Wood & Essien-Wood, 2012).

It is important to note that the coverage of potential theoretical frameworks in this chapter is not exhaustive. Moreover, readers should be directed to two additional resources that address other Black male educational frameworks. The first is Howard-Hamilton's (1997) overview of four developmental frameworks for African American men. In particular, this work provides descriptions of Cross's (1991) Nigrescence Theory as well as Robinson and Howard-Hamilton's (1994) Africentric Resistance Model. While these theories are more specific to the general Black experience, she noted that they provide effective insight into the more distinct educational realities of Black men. Second, and more directly pertinent to this chapter, we strongly encourage readers to access *Frameworks and Models of Black Male Success: A Guide for P-12 and Postsecondary Educators* (see Bonner, 2014b). This volume provides an extensive overview of theoretical frameworks relevant to Black men, covering a plethora of topical areas: gifted education; economically disadvantaged, high-achieving men; athletes; and gay men (among numerous other topics). In providing a value-added contribution to scholarship in this area, we have attempted to avoid frameworks covered in the works of Howard-Hamilton and Bonner.

THEORETICAL FRAMEWORKS

Presenting models and theories applicable to the Black male experience in postsecondary education is a particularly salient contribution to the scholarly literature. Specifically, given the exponential increase of research on Black men in education, this population has been strikingly both under-theorized and inadequately theorized in prior scholarship. As such, the models presented in this chapter serve as a collection of research lenses that we recommend for use as theoretical frameworks for future inquiry. Theory is the lifeblood of social science investigation, providing direction in nearly all empirical areas of inquiry (e.g., pure research, applied research, exploratory research, program evaluation). Theory has numerous benefits, helping to predict future phenomena, classifying existing phenomena, and providing insight into relationships between constructs (among other benefits). While there are numerous definitions of theory, we are inclined to Kerlinger's (1986) description. Kerlinger stated that theory is "a set of interrelated constructs, definitions, and propositions that presents a systemic view of phenomena by specifying relations among variables, with the purpose of explaining and predicting phenomena" (p. 64).

Theory can serve differing functions in inquiry-driven processes. For instance, pure quantitative research is deductive in nature. Given this, the focus of the investigation itself is (generally) to test the applicability of theory. In contrast, qualitative research tends to be inductive; as such, theory serves as a guiding lens for which results are interpreted. While theory can inform and be tested in research, theory can also be integral to informing practice (and practice can inform theory). Specifically, in a program-planning and evaluation context, theoretical frameworks can inform the development of program theories that undergird why programs have certain services, preventions, and interventions. When a theory is applied as the basis for research, this theory becomes a theoretical framework (Sevilla, Ochave, Punsalan, Regala, & Uriarte, 1992). Please note here that we are using the term theory in the most liberal sense, including the testing of claims (un-validated suppositions based on experiential knowledge and/or initial findings) and warranted assertions ('battle-tested' assertions based on extensive prior research). A theoretical framework is a theory (loosely defined) that can be applied as a lens to provide structure to express relationships and interactions between key variables, constructs, and phenomena. More simply, Merriam (1998) noted that a theoretical framework articulates the theoretical stance that a researcher brings to their study.

We should note that theoretical frameworks differ from process frameworks that have been developed for Black men. Process frameworks provide direction on how to engage in a given activity. Three salient examples of process frameworks include: Harper's (2010) anti-deficit achievement framework; Harper and Kuykendall's (2012) eight standards for institutional efforts to improve Black male achievement; and Holmes, Ebbers, Robinson, and Mugenda's (2007) model of Black male recruit. The first, Harper's (2010) anti-deficit model, is an example of a process framework for conducting research on Black men. Specifically, Harper (2010; 2012) provides lines of question that can be employed to avoid a deficit-oriented positioning of Black men in science, technology, engineering, and mathematics (STEM). For instance, a deficit question would include "Why are Black male undergraduates so disengaged in campus leadership positions and out-of-class activities?" while an anti-deficit achievement reframing would ask "What compelled Black male students to pursue leadership and engagement opportunities on their campuses?" (p. 68).

Harper outlines anti-deficit achievement areas of inquiry in three primary areas: precollege socialization and readiness (e.g., familial factors, K-12 forces, out-of-school college preparation), college achievement (e.g., classroom interactions, out-of-class engagement, experiential/external opportunities), and post-college persistence (e.g., industry, graduate school, research careers). An important benefit of this process framework is that it can be used in conjunction with asset-focused theories to explore the academic lives of Black men. Undoubtedly, much of our thinking about 'acceptable' ways to approach research on Black males in education (and students of color in general) is informed by Harper's anti-deficit achievement reframing.

The latter two examples, Harper and Kuykendall (2012) and Holmes et al. (2007) are process frameworks for programming and practice relevant to Black men. Harper and Kuykendall's (2012) framework provides a list of eight standards that should guide institutional efforts designed to foster positive outcomes for Black men. Examples of these eight standards include: "Black undergraduate men are meaningfully engaged as collaborators and viewed as experts in designing, implementing, and assessing campus initiatives" (p. 25); "Learning, academic achievement, student development, and improved degree attainment rates are prioritized over social programming" (p. 26); and "At every level, institutional agents are held accountable for improving Black male student retention, academic success, engagement, and graduation rates" (p. 28). These eight standards are guideposts for discerning 'good' practice in advancing outcomes for Black men in postsecondary education. Practitioners can use these standards to help identify challenges facing Black men, create interventions for this population, and to monitor the success of those interventions.

In addition to the aforementioned information about ways colleges could more effectively serve Black males, a model proposed by Holmes et al. (2007) provides a process framework relative to the recruitment of Black male students. This model is premised on elements from the Learning Outcomes Model advanced by Terenzini, Springer, Pascarella, and Nora (1995). Specifically, Holmes et al.'s (2007) model discusses how colleges and universities can support and validate minority students from entry until graduation. More specifically, Holmes et al. explain that the intent of this model was to demonstrate how the college environment could be reorganized to better facilitate students' educational experiences using tenets of Rendón's (1994) theory of validation. Holmes and colleagues posit that the model places greater influence on the institution influence on the student's academic outcomes as opposed to the student's pre-entry attributes because evidence suggests that what happens to students after they enter college has a stronger impact on their success than other factors. Despite this, Holmes et al. note that some students' pre-entry characteristics will impact how they progress through college as well as the kinds of activities with which they become engaged. Holmes et al.'s model consists of three stages. The first stage is validating students during the recruitment process. She and colleagues noted that institutions could more effectively recruit Black students by "creating a non-threatening and supportive environment where the prospective student and their outside validating agents (e.g., parents and/or significant others, etc.) can ask questions about the university without feeling intimidated because of his or her cultural group differences" (p. 51). Holmes et al. elucidate that students who feel valued at the recruitment stage are more likely to begin their careers at the college or university because "they belong and matter to the institution" (p. 51). The second stage emphasizes validating students through orientation as well as their first year experience in college. A critical aspect of this stage includes using opportunities inside and outside the classroom to validate and support students (see Table 3.1).

The final stage of Holmes et al.'s (2007) model emphasizes conducting an exit interview as students graduate to gain a better understanding of what policies and practices work and which ones need to be modified to better support students. They emphasize that colleges and universities should provide an exit interview to minority students upon graduation. This interview should serve to document the experiences of minority students in order to help the institution evaluate or modify retention strategies designed to support the success of all students, particularly Black male students. Holmes and colleagues suggested that the information gleaned from these assessments could be shared with university leaders to help them in their endeavor to create a positive campus climate for all

Table 3.1 Guided by Holmes et al.'s Model, Summary of Steps Colleges and Universities should Implement to Recruit and Support Black Males

Validation in the recruitment stage	Validating Black males inside and outside the Classroom	Exit Interviews
Colleges and universities should ensure that students and their validating agents (i.e., family) encounter friendly, supportive, and cultural competent faculty, staff, and administrators as students visit campus during the recruitment stage.	Upon matriculating, colleges and universities need to emphasize the importance of validating students inside and outside the classroom. This can occur through the following: • Emphasizing the importance of faculty to partner with student affairs practitioners to better understand how they could incorporate validation strategies into their pedagogical practices. Further, encouraging faculty to go beyond lecturing to actively engage students in the learning process while providing support and validation. Underscoring the importance of faculty having meaningful interactions with students inside and outside the classroom. • Establishing mentor initiatives on campus and linking students to professor, administrator, upperclassmen, or community member to experience support and validation outside the classroom. • Implementing Black male initiatives to help provide an additional opportunity for support and validating. • Partnering with students' families to provide an additional outlet for support and validation. • Providing ongoing college success workshops to further promote and provide opportunities for support and validation. • Implementing learning communities as an additional form of support and validation for Black male students.	Conduct exit interviews at the department level as students graduate. Information gleaned from this endeavor could be used to better understand effective policies and initiatives that helps promote success. Additionally, one year after students graduate, they should be contacted to participate in qualitative or quantitative assessments about their experience at the institution. Information from this initiative should be shared with institutional leaders to aid them in improving the campus climate for Black students.

students. To provide context to the central focus of this chapter (highlighting frameworks), the next section discusses the use of theoretical frameworks in prior research on Black men.

INADEQUATE USE OF FRAMEWORKS

To a large degree, the community of inquirers exploring the experiences of Black men in colleges and universities has espoused that they have a unique socio-cultural positioning that is distinctive to being both Black and male (see Bush & Bush, 2013a). As such, scholars (e.g., Bonner, 2014b; Bush & Bush, 2013b) have called for the use of theories and models that are specific to the Black male experience in education. Wood (2013) has even argued that, given differences in background characteristics between Black men in differing institutional types, the unique experiences of Black men are further distinguished by the institutions (e.g., community colleges, public four-year, private four-year) they attend. Given this, he calls for even more specific models and theories appropriate to the Black male experience in specific institutional contexts.

Despite this fact, researchers have largely ignored extant frameworks, models, and theories that were designed specifically for Black male (or male of color) populations in exchange for more predominant higher education theories. This is an important point, as theoretical frameworks are unscored by assumptions that permeate the research process. When not appropriate to the population of interest, these assumptions can serve to skew the research, impacting the quality and usefulness of study findings. Remember here that we previously noted that one important use of theory is to predict future phenomena; thus, weak theorizing can result in weak predictive utility.

For example, Wood (2010) conducted an analysis of theoretical frameworks employed to examine Black male students in community colleges. He examined 50 studies conducted between 1971 and 2009 on Black men in community colleges. Wood found that a number of studies were inhibited by weak theorizing, where theoretical frameworks were either underemployed (not used to scaffold the study or interpret results) or completely absent. Of the studies he examined, only 27 had clearly articulated frameworks. Moreover, of the 27 frameworks identified, 4 were used by multiple researchers: (a) Bandura's (1986; 1995; 1996) social learning theory (including concept of self-efficacy); (b) Bean and Metzner's (1985) model of nontraditional student attrition; (c) Tinto's (1975, 1987, 1988, 1993) retention/departure theory/model; and (d) critical theory, including Critical Race Theory (CRT) (Bell, 1980). With the exception of CRT and one study that used Carroll's (1988) model of Black freshman retention, no studies examined employed frameworks focused on Black student populations. Furthermore, none of the studies identified used a theoretical framework specific to the Black male experience.

In contrast, the vast majority of scholars relied on traditional frameworks (i.e., Bandura, 1986; Tinto, 1975; Bean & Metzner, 1985). Wood noted that this was a particularly concerning trend given that scholars (e.g., Mason, 1998) had created retention models specific to Black men in community colleges that had yet to be employed at that time. To be clear, using predominant frameworks can be appropriate for many studies. Research from student integration (e.g., Tinto, 1975), nontraditional student attrition (Bean & Metzner, 1985), involvement (Astin, 1993), sense of belonging (Strayhorn, 2012), Critical Race Theory (Bell, 1980; Solórzano, 1998), validation (Rendón, 1994), and campus racial climate (Hurtado & Carter, 1997) among other works in the higher education canon can provide strong theoretical underpinning for research. In fact, our own research has relied heavily upon these frameworks to guide our conceptualization and interpretation of phenomena (e.g., Palmer et al., 2011; Palmer & Maramba, 2011; Wood, 2012a–c). However, if Black men do indeed have a distinct socio-cultural positioning (Bush & Bush, 2013a), then these theories may not fully address the nuances of their realities, identities, and experiences. As such, population-specific frameworks are necessary to lend insight into the unique lives of these men. Given this, the focus of the next section is to present five theoretical frameworks that we believe present viable alternatives when predominant theories used in educational research do not provide enough specificity.

FIVE THEORETICAL FRAMEWORKS ON BLACK MEN

In this section, we present African American Male Theory (Bush & Bush, 2013a), the Socio-Ecological Outcomes (SEO) model (Harris & Wood, in press), Expressions of Spirituality (Herndon, 2003), Prove-Them-Wrong Syndrome (Moore et al., 2003), and Capital Identity Projection (Wood & Essien-Wood, 2012). These theories were selected since they were developed with a specific focus on Black men (or men of color). Here, we have attempted to portray a wide range of theories addressing the scholarly thought on Black men.

African American Male Theory

Bush and Bush (2013a; 2013b) introduced African American Male Theory (AAMT), a meta-level theory for understanding the lives of Black men. Specifically, they proffer AAMT as a theoretical framework to "articulate the position and trajectory of African American boys and men in society" (Bush & Bush, 2013a, p. 6). They situate the theory as a development in men's studies literature, but also emanating from several traditions, including: African-centered Theory, Critical Race Theory, and Womanist Theory. The theory itself is comprised of six primary tenets that serve as guiding principles for inquiry relevant to the experience of Black boys and men.

The first tenet of AAMT acknowledges that the lived socio-cultural realities (e.g., experiences, perceptions, outcomes) of Black men "are best analyzed using an ecological systems approach" (p. 7). In particular, they highlight Bronfenbrenner's (1989) ecological systems theory and the African worldview as predominant informants of the ecological approach. With regard to Bronfenbrenner's work, they argue that the interconnectedness of systems (e.g., micro-system, meso-system, exo-system, macro-system, chrono-system) shapes the lives of Black boys and men. A key derivation from Bronfenbrenner is that they divide the micro-system into two distinct categories, the inner micro-system (inclusive of biology, personality, beliefs, and perceptions) and the outer micro-system (including one's family, extended family, home, and peers). Among other modifications, they also proffer a new system, the sub-system, which recognizes the supernatural, spiritual, and collective unconsciousness of Black men.

The second tenet of AAMT recognizes the distinctive realities of "being male and of African descent" (p. 10). As such, they note that AAMT is concerned with discovering and evidencing the unique lives, experiences, and perceptions of Black men. They suggest that documenting these distinctions requires cross-disciplinary perspectives that can result in programming and practices that are distinct to Black men across numerous contexts (e.g., education, healthcare).

Third, AAMT follows in the Afrocentric tradition by asserting that "there is a continuity and continuation of African culture, consciousness, and biology" in the lives of Black boys and men (p. 10). Simply put, they assert that the study of Black men should be "anchored in Africa." As such, they argue that Black culture, biology, and spirituality can be inextricably linked to pre-colonial Africa.

The fourth tenet of AAMT is that "African American boys and men are resilient and resistant" (p. 10). They highlight resilience theory as an important component of AAMT that should be understood in light of the ecological systems approach proffered in their first tenet. In making this assertion, they state that self-determination is 'innate' to Black men. They suggest that this point runs counter to predominant stereotypes of Black men that portray them as biologically and culturally deficient. For instance, they argue that John Ogbu's (1991) work on 'acting White' is an example of resistance and resilience. Ogbu argued that African Americans reject education for fear of 'acting White'. Specifically, they noted that Ogbu wrongly conceptualized education and schooling as synonymous; instead they noted that African Americans reject schooling that is typified by asymmetries of power. In this light, Black men reject subjugation by which schooling is a vehicle, not education itself.

Fifth, AAMT espouses that "race and racism coupled with classism and sexism have a profound impact" on the lives of Black men (p. 11). They note that this perspective emanates from Critical Race Theory (CRT), recognizing that racism is omnipresent in American life and society. Key to this tenet is that they prioritize

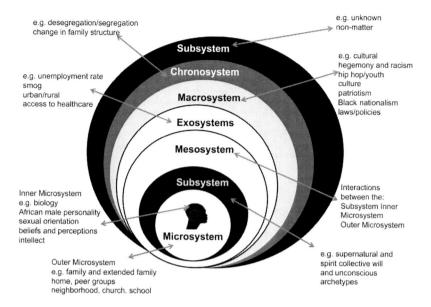

e.g. desegregation/segregation change in family structure

e.g. unknown non-matter

Subsystem

Chronosystem

e.g. unemployment rate smog urban/rural access to healthcare

e.g. cultural hegemony and racism hip hop/youth culture patriotism Black nationalism laws/policies

Macrosystem

Exosystems

Mesosystem

Subsystem

Inner Microsystem e.g. biology African male personality sexual orientation beliefs and perceptions intellect

Interactions between the: Subsystem Inner Microsystem Outer Microsystem

Microsystem

Outer Microsystem e.g. family and extended family home, peer groups neighborhood. church. school

e.g. supernatural and spirit collective will and unconscious archetypes

Figure 3.1 African American Male Ecological Systems Model for African American Male Theory.

Used with permission from Lawson Bush V and Edward C. Bush © 2013.

race and the intersection of race with class and gender above other forms of marginality (e.g., disability, religion, sexual orientation).

Finally, the sixth tenet of AAMT is the "pursuit of social justice" (p. 12). They note that the research and practice relevant to the lives of Black boys and men should be social justice-oriented in nature. As such, programming that does not aim to improve the life outcomes of Black boys and men is portrayed as hegemonic.

Socio-Ecological Outcomes Model

Also drawing from scholarly thought in human ecology, Harris and Wood (in press) and Wood and Harris (2012) articulated the Socio-Ecological Outcomes (SEO) model. The SEO model is an outgrowth of Harris and Wood's Five Domains of African American Male Student Success in Community Colleges. This model focuses on the nexus of social and ecological planes to portray factors that influence success outcomes (e.g., persistence, achievement, attainment, transfer) for men who have been historically underrepresented and underserved in education, particularly men of color (see Figure 3.1). The model has most explicit utility for community colleges, as the model was created and had initial validation work done on men of color (particularly Black and Latino men) in community colleges. The model is principally informed by Bensimon's (2007) concepts of equity-mindedness and institutional responsibility, which places the responsibility for student success on the institutions, as opposed to the student. Moreover, SEO adheres to the Inputs, Environment, and Outputs (IEO) structure set forth by Astin (1993). According to Astin, the success and development of students in educational programming fall into three areas: inputs, the background and defining characteristics students bring with them into educational programming; environment, the experiences students have in the educational program; and outputs, the development and success factors that result from the interaction of inputs and environment. Similarly, Harris and Wood's model is divided into three distinct areas of consideration: (a) precollege considerations (referred to as inputs); (b) experiences that occur during college (referred to as domains); and (c) students' success outputs (referred to as outcomes).

Harris and Wood (in press) identify two primary factors that shape precollege experiences for men of color; they include background and defining factors and societal factors. Background and defining factors include characteristics such as their age, time status (part-time, full-time attendance), veteran status, primary language, citizenship status, generation status, and (dis)ability. For instance, they note that men of color who attend college part-time are less likely to experience success than those who attend full-time. Societal factors include stereotypes about men of color, prejudice they face in societal, economic conditions, and capital identity projection (described separately in this chapter). Both background and defining factors as well as societal factors shape the experiences of men of color as they encounter college environments.

During college, the authors identified four primary factors that influence the success of men of color (as shaped by the precollege inputs). These factors are referred to as socio-ecological domains and they include: non-cognitive, academic, environmental, and campus ethos domains. The authors postulate that the campus ethos and environmental domains have an effect on the academic and non-cognitive domains, whereas the latter domains (e.g., academic, non-cognitive) have a bidirectional relationship with one another. Collectively, for men of color these four domains influence persistence, achievement, attainment, transfer, goal attainment, and initial labor market outcomes.

The environmental domain is inclusive of factors that occur outside of college that have an impact on student success inside of college. Such environmental factors include commitments (e.g., familial obligations, employment), stressful life events (e.g., divorce, death in family, eviction, incarceration), and external mediators (e.g., college-related validation from family and peers, financial aid, transportation). Environmental factors typically fall outside the direct locus of influence of colleges and universities, but are critical to student success. The campus ethos domain is comprised of several essential factors, including: internal

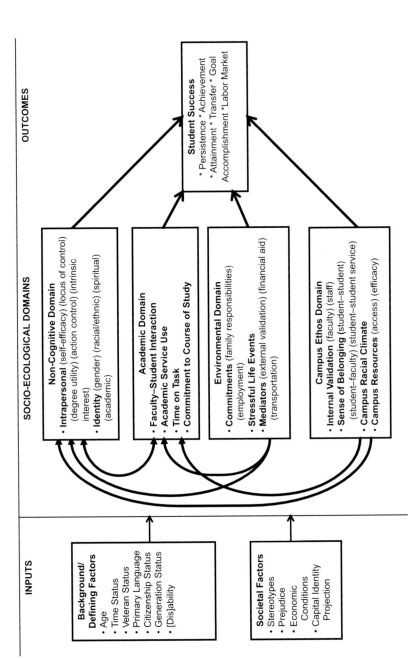

Figure 3.2 The Socio-Ecological Outcomes Model by Harris and Wood.

validation from faculty and staff; sense of belonging as it relates to other students, faculty, and student service staff; students' perceptions of connectedness to the general campus environment; and students' access and perceived efficacy of campus resources. All factors within the campus ethos domains fall within colleges' locus of influence, and situate the onus of student success as an institutional responsibility.

As noted, both the campus ethos and environmental domains affect the academic and non-cognitive domains. The academic domains are inclusive of students' academic experiences, such as their interaction with faculty, use of academic services on campus (e.g., computer lab, academic advising, career counseling, tutoring services), and their commitment to their course of study or other goals (broadly defined). This domain has an interactive relationship with the non-cognitive domains, which is divided into two areas: intrapersonal factors and identity factors. Intrapersonal factors are psychosocial in nature, including students' self-efficacy (confidence in their ability to succeed academically), locus of control (sense of control over their academic futures), degree utility (perception of the worthwhileness of college), action control (directed attention or focus on academic endeavors), and intrinsic interest (inherent rewards reaped from their studies). Identity factors focus the role of one's masculine, racial, spiritual, and academic identity in one's success. These factors are a core element of the model, which note that students' success cannot be conceptualized irrespective of the unique ways in which men interpret, interiorize, and execute their unique identities.

Expressions of Spirituality

While Harris and Wood (in press) noted that spirituality was an important element of the identities of men of color, other research has advanced this notion as central to understanding Black male success. Spirituality is a core element of Black life and culture. Spirituality and religion influence the ways in which many individuals of African descent experience and negotiate social institutions (Mattis, 2000; 2004). Drawing upon this notion, Herndon (2003) examined the influence of spirituality on the academic lives of Black men at a four-year institution. From interviews with 13 Black men, Herndon extended that there were 3 primary ways (or expressions) in which Black men noted that spirituality supported their persistence in college. Similar to Moore and colleagues' (2003) work on proving-them-wrong, Herndon (2003) noted that his three expressions of spirituality served as a coping mechanism for men who face academic and social barriers.

The first expression of spirituality was resilience. Herndon noted that spirituality served as a resilience factor for Black men. He discussed how religious activities such as prayer, attending religious services, and reading scriptures helped Black men to overcome challenges they faced (e.g., racism, stereotypes) and to reduce their stress. Second, Herndon noted that spirituality provided Black men with "a sense of purpose, direction, and focus in life" (p. 80). Herndon noted that spirituality informed their academic goals, providing men with a greater level of commitment to their academic pursuits. Black men in his study noted that their purpose in life was directed by God; thus, spirituality heightened the importance and internalization of their goals. The third expression of spirituality was religious institutional support. Herndon noted that, due to their religious connections and relationships, Black men received support in college from religious institutional members. Specifically, these men received personal encouragement to continue in college.

In 2008, Riggins, McNeal, and Herndon conducted a replication study of Herndon's prior work. Largely, findings from their study produced results similar to the original study. For instance, they found that spirituality was a resilience factor for Black men. They emphasized that prayer served as a core coping mechanism. They also found that prayer provided students with a sense of connection to their life purpose and that Black men received support from churches. However, they extended on the prior study, adding an additional expression of spirituality. They found that spirituality enabled Black men to receive social support from other Black men. Specifically, they noted that Black men verbalized their spiritual beliefs to one another and that these beliefs heightened a common bond that they had with other Black men. Collectively, Herndon's works present four expressions of spirituality, noting that spirituality fosters resilience, a sense of purpose, support from church bodies, and social connectedness to other Black men.

Prove-Them-Wrong Syndrome

While AAMT (Bush & Bush, 2013a) and the Expressions of Spirituality (Herndon, 2003) elaborated on the importance of resilience, other research has articulated why and how resilience facilitates Black male success. In 2003, Moore et al. introduced the Prove-Them-Wrong Syndrome, which they extended as an explanatory theoretical framework for understanding Black male persistence in STEM fields (particularly engineering). The Prove-Them-Wrong Syndrome was an outgrowth of a qualitative study with 24 Black male juniors and seniors who were engineering majors. These men were selected for participation in the study because they overcame potential barriers by persisting to the latter levels of undergraduate study. Using a grounded theory approach, data were collected from participants via a biographical questionnaire, individual interviews, and focus groups. Their findings produced an 'emergent theory' that provided insight into why Black men were able to persist in an environment rife with perceptions of Black inferiority.

Our interpretation of the Prove-Them-Wrong Syndrome suggests that there are four primary components of the theory, which we refer to as structural conditions, affective disposition, intended outcome, and affective response. The syndrome occurs when four interrelated negative structural conditions are evident. First, Prove-Them-Wrong Syndrome is situated in academic fields not traditionally associated with African American men (such as engineering). Second, actual underrepresentation of Black men in the field of focus must be prevalent at the institution. Third, the syndrome is manifested when the institutional climate is rife with stereotypes regarding the intellectual inferiority of Black men, particularly from White faculty and students. Fourth, Black men in the field of focus must have awareness of the negative stereotypes about them in the field. To be clear, Moore and colleagues noted that Black men in their study had an acute awareness of stereotypes about their intellectual abilities (see Claude Steele's (1997) work on stereotype threat). The Prove-Them-Wrong Syndrome explains how these men overcame these stereotypes.

A unifying affective disposition evident in Black men with the Prove-Them-Wrong Syndrome is that they have direct control over the outcomes of their academic futures. In other words, men with the syndrome illustrate high internal locus of causality. The aim for men with this disposition in structural conditions rife with stereotypes and underrepresentation is to counteract these narratives. Men with the Prove-Them-Wrong Syndrome aim at proving naysayers wrong, especially those who doubt their abilities and belonging in underrepresented fields. The aim is fueled by affective responses to inimical structural conditions. The affective responses can be classified as a coping mechanism to aid in overcoming perceived barriers. The responses identified by Moore and colleagues are wide-ranging, including positive vigor, enhanced motivation, increased commitment to their course of study, enhanced self-confidence (academic self-efficacy), greater determination, improved work ethic, and a clearer sense of their academic purpose. Collectively, these affective responses enable Black men to work harder to reach their intended goals.

Capital Identity Projection

While the aforementioned frameworks have grounded the Black experience, they typically overlook root mechanisms that lead to deleterious outcomes for Black men. For example, two students receive financial aid, one student will choose to spend it on buying books and paying for his housing, while another may use the monies to purchase new rims for his car. Understanding these choices requires a view on Black men from the lens of economic psychology. Wood and Essien-Wood (2012) extended the concept of Capital Identity Projection, to describe how capitalism fosters negative outcomes for Black males. Capital Identity Projection is a harmful psychosocial disposition resulting from capitalistic value systems that occurs when individuals pursue an image of economic success to the point of their own detriment.

The concept emerged from a qualitative grounded theory research study of the experiences of 29 Black male collegians.[1] Individuals displaying these actions are referred to as projectors because they were concerned about publicly presenting an image of success fueled by capitalistic values. Specifically, Wood and Essien-Wood noted that "this projection is a by-product of a capitalistic value system where mores of individualism, glory-seeking, and economic success are fostered and idealized as a proxy for happiness, self-worth, and life achievement" (p. 987). They argued that the conflation of these ideals is fostered, framed, and propagated through the media in order to spur individual spending. Wood and Essien-Wood asserted that there are four primary, interrelated premises associated with Capital Identity Projection theory: (a) an overstated image of success is pursued irrationally; (b) there is an erroneous conflation of capital attainment, self-worth, and happiness; (c) the notions of glory-seeking, consumerism, and materialism are interiorized; and (d) projection is a direct result of capitalist value systems and resultant marketing enterprises. We address each of these notions individually.

The first premise of Capital Identity Projection is that there is an irrational pursuit of a capital image. They noted that men in their study purchased goods (e.g., clothing, jewelry, cars) for the primary purpose of displaying these goods for others to see. The purpose of displaying these goods was to project an image of status attainment. Wood and Essien-Wood noted that the capital image can be pursued irrationally, with *some* individuals placing the image of success before their own basic needs (e.g., paying bills for housing and electricity), and endangering their goals (e.g., personal, career, academic). Moreover, they noted that because women are often objectified through capitalistic marketing systems (e.g., video girls), they can be viewed as akin to goods, where individuals collect and display women to maintain a capital image.

The second premise is that individuals conflate the concepts of capital attainment, happiness, and self-worth. Specifically, they stated that perceptions of worth and happiness are inextricably tied to ownerships of goods. These goods are sought without respect for delayed gratification. The third premise articulated by Wood and Essien-Wood is that glory-seeking, materialism, and consumerism are interiorized. They used the word 'interiorized' to connote the inner integration of these values into the inner being. They associated the interiorizing of these values with capitalistic value systems that associate status with consumerism. They noted that the interiorizing of these values can detract from other pursuits (e.g., academic, career) as individuals' focus is on an image of capital attainment. Thus, *some* men spent more time displaying an image of success through clothing, being flashy, and attention-seeking actions as opposed to academically necessary habits (e.g., studying, using support services).

The fourth and final premise of Capital Identity Projection is that individuals engaged in these actions are merely a by-product of resultant socialization perpetuated by a capitalist value system through its marketing enterprise (e.g., television, radio, magazine, videos). They noted that the value system espouses the values identified in the third premise (e.g., glory-seeking, materialism, consumerism) in excess in order to sustain the function of the economic system. Moreover, they noted that the capitalist marketing enterprises "access and shape archetypes and stereotypes around identity in order to foster materialism and facilitate consumerism" (p. 992). The system itself keys in on, shapes, extends, and inculcates a fabricated portrayal of identity (e.g., racial, masculine) in order to ensure that purchasing patterns continue to occur. In essence, Black men (like others in capitalistic societies) are indoctrinated to pursue irrational courses of action that support the economic base.

There are several important points to note in contextualizing Capital Identity Projection. First, Wood and Essien-Wood noted that this malady is the result of a capitalistic value system and its resultant socialization and is not innate to the individuals who display this behavior. Second, they noted that Capital Identity Projection is endemic to all communities in society, but that the capitalist marketing enterprise keys in on and fabricates identities (both positive and negative) that are unique to specific groups such as Black men. Third, they noted that, while some scholars would attribute Capital Identity Projection to being 'cool' or 'cool pose,' the root cause of individual actions is not authentic culture, but shaped to support the capitalist value system.

CONCLUDING REMARKS

Collectively, these frameworks acknowledged the role that stereotypes, race, and racism have in the lives of Black men in general and in academic contexts (Bush & Bush, 2013a; Harris & Wood, in press; Herndon, 2003; Moore et al., 2003; Wood & Essien-Wood, 2012). Bush and Bush (2013a) and Harris and Wood (in press) characterized racism as being endemic to society, while Herndon (2003) suggested that spirituality served as a resilient factor against racism. In like manner, Moore et al. (2003) argued that the Prove-Them-Wrong Syndrome emerged in climates rife with racism and stereotypes. From a different perspective, Wood and Essien-Wood (2012) articulated the economic base that produced racism and stereotypes, suggesting that capitalist marketing enterprises shape stereotypes about Black men in order to foster consumerism and materialism.

Several core themes were evident across these frameworks. First, the models highlighted the integral role that locus of control has on Black male success. For example, high internal locus of control was identified by Harris and Wood (in press) as a facilitator of male of color success, while Moore et al. (2003) noted that men with a feeling of direct control over the outcomes of their academic futures illustrated resilience by proving others wrong. Spirituality was another common theme evident throughout the frameworks' highlights; while Herndon (2003) most clearly articulated the role that spirituality has in bolstering academic success, the importance of spirituality in the lives of men was also addressed by Bush and Bush (2013a) via the sub-system and by Harris and Wood (in press) as an identity element. The concept of resilience and resistance was imbedded across most of the models. Bush and Bush (2013a) argued that resilience is inherent to Black men, while Herndon (2003) suggested that spirituality served as a core driver for resilience. Moore et al. (2003) extended upon this understanding of resilience by noting that it can be manifested via the Prove-Them-Wrong Syndrome.

As noted in this chapter, there are many predominant frameworks (e.g., integration, belonging, CRT) that have utility for examining the lives of Black men in college. However, guided by the assumption that Black male experience is distinct yet nuanced within-group (Bush & Bush, 2013a), there are some instances when more specific models and theories are needed that account for the unique racial, gender, and cultural realities of this group. In this chapter, we presented five frameworks that can be used to research Black men in postsecondary education. These frameworks can serve to guide researchers in reframing their thinking, avoiding irrelevant assumptions, and uncovering new insights that can bolster the success of Black men. In the next chapter, we explicate a new model for understanding the success of Black men. The model approaches student success from an institutional responsibility vantage point. We believe a theoretical transition toward a greater focus on the institutions' role in student success is necessary for the next generation of research and practice focused on Black males in postsecondary education.

NOTE

1   Though the nuances of Capital Identity Projection are described with specific focus on *some* Black men, they stated that the actions are not acute to this population, but to all individuals under the inimical effect of capitalistic value systems.

Chapter 4

The Context, Actions, and Outcomes (CAO) Model of Institutional Responsibility

Every system is perfectly designed to achieve the results it gets.
(attributed to W. Edward Deming and to Paul Batalden)

In 1975, Vincent Tinto's article "Dropouts from higher education: A synthesis of recent research" was published in the *Review of Educational Research*. This article, as well as similar arguments in his subsequent works (see Tinto, 1987; 1988; 1993) has served as foundational sociological explanations for student attrition and retention in college. As briefly discussed in Chapter 3, Tinto has suggested that student success should be viewed from a longitudinal lens. For him, student persistence was a result of interactions between the student and the social and academic systems of the college or university they attend. According to Tinto, as students transition into a college, they become acquainted with and enveloped in the academic and social milieu of college. As a result of their interactions, students assert and evaluate their core commitment to the institution. Continuous interactions serve to shape students' academic paths and goals. Tinto postulated that students with greater levels of integration into the campus academic and social systems will experience greater degrees of commitment to the institution, and increase their likelihood of persistence and completion. This theory has been widely used in research on Black men to articulate the importance of these students becoming integrated into the campus milieu (Flowers, 2006; Hagedorn, Maxwell & Hampton, 2001–2002; Ray, Carly, & Brown, 2009). In fact, in our own work, we have drawn explicitly or implicitly from this framework (Palmer et al., 2011; Palmer, Davis, & Thompson, 2010; Wood, 2012a–c). The theory is also regularly pointed to by academic and student affairs leaders to justify co-curricular activities, extracurricular activities, leadership development, and academic programming that provide avenues for increased integration into a college environment.

In the past two decades, scholars have become increasingly critical of this framework for several reasons. First, some have noted that the theory is imbedded with an expectation that students should and must 'break away' from their families and their communities to be successful in college (Guiffrida, 2006; Hurtado, Carter, & Spuler, 1996; Nora & Cabrera, 1996; Palmer et al., 2011). In this light, Tinto stated "in order to become fully incorporated in the life of the college, [students] have to physically as well as socially dissociate themselves from the communities of the past" (Tinto, 1993, p. 96). These scholars have suggested that disconnection from one's community, especially for historically disadvantaged students, fosters disconnection and isolation, not collegiate success. Second, other scholars have critiqued Tinto's work, suggesting that the focus of his analysis is on the student and how the student integrates into the institution (Johnson, Soldner, Leonard, Alvarez, Inkelas, Rowan-Kenyon, & Longerbeam, 2007; Tierney, 1992). For instance, Tinto (1987) stated "the problems associated with separation and transition to college are conditions that, though stressful, need not in themselves lead to departure. It is the individual's response to those conditions that finally determines staying or leaving" (p. 98). As a result, scholars have charged that this theory places the onus for student success on the student themselves, not the institutions that serve them (Johnson et al., 2007). As noted by Rendón, Jalomo, and Nora (2000), Tinto's theory propagates the notion that "individuals, not the system, are responsible for departure" (p. 144).

The latter critique, while evident in Tinto's work, is also apparent in concepts by subsequent works focused on quality of student effort and student engagement. For instance, Pace (1980; 1984; 1985; 1990) is credited with establishing the College Student Experiences Questionnaire (CSEQ). The theoretical undergirding of this instrument is his concept of 'quality of effort,' which postulated that students who invested greater levels of time, focus, and energy into their studies and interacting with others (e.g., student, faculty) were more likely to succeed. This notion is the antecedent of the contemporary concept of engagement, which according to Kuh (2003) is "used to represent constructs such as quality of effort and involvement in productive learning activities" (p. 6). Hereto, the focus of analysis is on what the student does to succeed in college, irrespective of the college's responsibility for educating the student. This perspective on student (not institutional) responsibility also intersects with Astin's (1993) theory of student involvement, a point we will revisit later in this chapter.

In departing from this line of inquiry, we sought to provide a framework in this chapter that would allow scholars and practitioners to focus on institutional responsibility for Black male success in college. Like the numerous constructs (background, societal, academic, social, environmental) traditionally espoused in research as affecting student success (e.g., persistence, achievement, attainment) from the students' locus of control, we sought to provide a comprehensive (though likely not exhaustive) account of the myriad of institutional domains affecting student success from the institutions' locus of control. We refer to these considerations as the eight key domains of institutional responsibility. The elements of these domains are in line with the increasing trajectory of research focused on the role of institutions in supporting student success (Bush & Bush, 2010; Harper, 2009). With respect to Black male achievement in college, Bush (2004) uses the biblical metaphor of the fig tree to connote this more progressive ideology. Bush sees students as akin to the fruit borne by a fig tree while the institution represents the tree itself. He suggests that if a tree produced bad fruit, the blame would be on the tree itself, not on the fruit. In like manner, when institutions produce poor student outcomes, it is illogical to suggest that the student outcomes are the sole responsibility of the student themselves. Rather, the institutions (fig trees) producing those student outcomes are viewed as having responsibility for their student outcomes (fruit). The next section discusses the philosophical perspective undergirding institutional responsibility praxis.

INSTITUTIONAL RESPONSIBILITY: BENSIMON'S COGNITIVE FRAMES

Institutional responsibility shifts the onus of student success from the student to the organization itself. To aid in understanding this philosophical shift, Bensimon (2005) articulates three primary cognitive frames that are employed around the notion of institutional responsibility for underserved student outcomes. She notes that cognitive frames are lenses or 'interpretive frameworks' by which individuals make meaning of phenomena. In the context of institutional responsibility, these frames include the deficit, diversity, and equity cognitive frames. The deficit cognitive framework has a focus on blaming students, their families, and their communities for inadequate student outcomes. The discourse for this frame centers on students' lack of preparedness, self-determination, and academic habits. This lens is oriented around stereotypical notions of poverty, race, and the 'culture of disadvantage.' As a result of this lens, the focus of educational programming is to remediate and fix the student. For example, the deficit cognitive frame suggests that the reason students are not doing well is because they come from schools and communities that do not value education nor have academic rigor. As a result, they are not ready for college and therefore must be remediated to fix what their high schools and parents should have done.

The second frame is the diversity cognitive frame. This frame is oriented around antiquated discourse on representational diversity among students. In this lens, student diversity is viewed as an important attribute of the institution, as exposure to diversity is a compelling interest to better educate majority students for a global marketplace. As such, educational programming centers on cultural sensitivity training and providing opportunities for majority students to engage students of color. As such, in this frame, Black men are provided access to college due to the inherent benefit they can provide for other students, not necessarily for the benefits they will personally derive. While the deficit and diversity cognitive frames predominate postsecondary education philosophy and educational practice, they lack true responsibility and accountability for underserved student outcomes. Instead, Bensimon (2005) argues that colleges and universities should employ equity cognitive frames.

Equity frames are oriented around a commitment to institutional programs, policies, and practices that foster disparate outcomes for historically underrepresented and underserved student communities. This frame takes a critical orientation, focusing on areas where disparities are evident and targeting resources in these areas to produce equitable outcomes. In this frame, educational programming is not focused on remediating students or exposing majority students to compositional diversity, but rather on changing the inherent organizational structures that limit student success. This involves assuming responsibility for student outcomes, challenging the deficit and diversity cognitive frames, and developing systems to monitor outcomes. In this frame, college professionals take responsibility for the discourse on underserved student success, including "institutional responsibility for student outcomes, the manifestation of institutionalized racism, color-conscious[ness], awareness of racialized practices and their differential consequences, [and] awareness of white privilege" (Bensimon, 2005, p. 103). Guided by these notions of responsibility, the next section presents key domains of action within the locus of control of postsecondary institutions.

MODEL OVERVIEW: CONTEXT, ACTIONS, AND OUTCOMES

Postsecondary institutions are often told that they must assume responsibility for student success. However, many college leaders are unclear as to what 'responsibility' or 'accountability' actually means. Some fear these words, believing they solely connote encroaching state and federal oversight despite declining resource trends. Others perceive recommendations for institutional responsibility as theoretically justifiable, but impractical given the numerous programs and students served. For these college leaders, institutional responsibility may be 'code' for increasing institutional resources to single sub-groups (e.g., Black men) who may represent a small proportion of their student bodies. Moreover, arguably the most common viewpoint expressed is one of external responsibility. Practitioners will often point to the role of factors in student environments (e.g., family responsibilities, work, stressful life events, transportation), noting that there is little (if anything) that institutions can do to mitigate the effect of these considerations on student success. We believe that when conversations on student success begin with the student, they shift the focus and onus of responsibility on students, their families, and the (PreK-12) schools they come from. When this occurs, discourse on institutional responsibility thereafter becomes the counter-argument, the antithesis, and the alternative argument. Instead, it is essential that practitioners and researchers alike begin discussions on Black male success by focusing on what the institution is, and is not doing, to support them. As noted by Harris, Bensimon, and Bishop (2010):

> it is futile to dwell on students' past experiences. It is also harmful if inequalities are rationalized as beyond the control of practitioners. [Instead] we must focus on what *is* within the control of educators in terms of changing their own practices to meet the needs and circumstances of men of color.
>
> (p. 280)

Bearing this in mind, we present the Context, Actions, and Outcomes (CAO) model. The CAO model focuses intently on the institutional responsibility for student success. The model takes into account the contextual aspects of the institution, the institution's actions and ethos to support student success, as well as the outcomes derived from those efforts. The model is juxtaposed to the student responsibility model espoused by Astin (1993). Like work from his contemporaries (e.g., Tinto, Kuh), we believe Astin's model erroneously places the onus of student success on the student. Specifically, Astin's IEO model contends that students enter into an institution of higher education with previous inputs (e.g., personal attributes, prior school experiences). Then, students engage in the campus 'environment' through involvement in academic and social matters and educational programming. This involvement then shapes the outcomes experienced by the student. Instead of focusing on students' inputs, the CAO model hones in on the institution's inputs (referred to as contextual factors). These contextual factors include the institutional history, revenue streams, location, size, and institutional type (e.g., community college, HBCU, PWI). All of these factors are foundational to the institution's mode of operation. In particular, institutional type is an essential consideration as core differences in mission (e.g., serving Black communities, serving local communities, serving state research interests), functions (e.g., remediation, certificates, degrees, transfer), and student populations served differ across institutional types.

The crux of the CAO model is the Actions—what Astin refers to as the 'environment.' Astin's (1993) work assumes that some students are more inclined to participate in certain experiences than others. In contrast, we assume that the institutional actions and ethos shape experiential realities within the institution. While students enter postsecondary education with differing backgrounds and experiences, the institution must respond to them 'where they are at.' In other words, we do not believe it is solely the students' responsibility to 'change' for their environment, but rather that the 'environment' should evolve to serve them. As a result, Actions encompass eight key domains of institutional responsibility for student success (discussed extensively in the next section). These

55

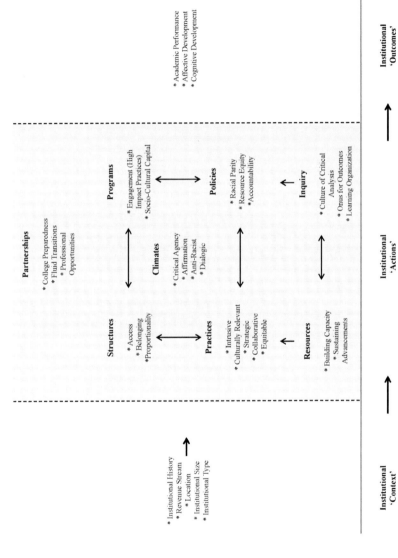

Figure 4.1 Context, Actions, and Outcomes (CAO) Model of Institutional Responsibility.

domains foster student affective development and academic performance outcomes (e.g., persistence, achievement, attainment). The responsibility for these outcomes falls within the domain of institutional responsibility, not the student inputs or student-pursued experiences in the environment. The central focus of the model is on the Actions of the institution. The next section describes the Action proffered in this model, which we have termed the eight domains of institutional responsibility.

ACTION: THE EIGHT DOMAINS OF INSTITUTIONAL RESPONSIBILITY

Conversations on institutional responsibility have addressed a number of key areas of concern (e.g., resources, data, messaging) (Bush & Bush, 2010; Edwards, Cangemi, & Kowalski, 1990; Harbour & Nagy, 2005; Wood & Hilton, 2012). Much of the work done in this area has focused on organizational learning as a strategy for increasing institutional capacity to serve historically underrepresented and underserved students (e.g., Bensimon, 2005; Kezar, 2005a). Within this literature base, our conceptualization of institutional responsibility is chiefly informed by the scholarship of Estella Bensimon (particularly her foundational work on the equity scorecard) and Shaun Harper (and his critical inquiry surrounding institutional responsibility for Black male success). Based on a synthesis of their findings, as well as other emergent research on institutional responsibility and accountability, organizational learning, college student success, and Black male achievement, we have identified eight key domains of institutional responsibility for Black male success. These eight interrelated domains of 'action' include: programs, policies, practices, resources, structures, climates, partnerships, and inquiry. These domains, as well as selected sub-domains and by-products (or results) are depicted in Table 4.1.

Each domain of institutional responsibility is intended to lead to the ultimate outcome, student success. Our perspective on institutional responsibility begins with the notion that institutions of postsecondary learning (e.g., community college, liberal arts college, HBCU, four-year university) assume responsibility for the students that are enrolled in their institutions. That is, once the student is enrolled, the college or university takes ownership of the student's affective development, cognitive development, and academic performance outcomes (e.g., persistence, achievement, attainment). Affective development refers to the emotional and dispositional growth of the student. The notion encapsulates their temperament, self-esteem, self-concept, and psychological well-being (Nevarez & Wood, 2010). Affective development is predicated on an academic and social learning environment that is affirming, supportive, and nurturing. These key elements provide a fertile environment where students can engage in discourse and experiences that allow them to learn more about themselves and others.

57

Cognitive development "accounts for the ways an individual develops critical thinking and reasoning processes" (Barr & Desler, 2000, p. 236). Cognitive development is a function of the formal and informal learning environment. In the classroom, students encounter new concepts, ideas, philosophies, and other content that challenges and extends their previous knowledge. However, as noted by Barr and Desler (2000), cognitive development also connotes the development of critical thinking and other higher order reasoning (e.g., evaluation, synthesis) that is the mark of a learned individual. As with a student's affective development, affirmation, support, and nurturance are necessary conditions for cognitive development. Institutions must take accountability for outcomes experienced by underserved student communities (Bensimon, 2005), particularly for Black males (Harper, 2009; Harper & Kuykendall, 2012). To be clear, colleges and universities are responsible for equitable outcomes (Bensimon, 2005) that close achievement gaps between Black men and their racial/ethnic and gender counterparts (Harper, 2006). Each of the eight domains portrays elements necessary to foster outcome parity.

Programs are the first key domain of institutional responsibility. Colleges and universities are responsible for providing high impact academic and co-curricular programming for all students, including Black men. Note here, that we emphasize academic and co-curricular programming as opposed to purely social programming. As noted by Harper and Kuykendall (2012) many colleges "focus almost entirely on providing entertainment and opportunities for social interaction among Black students" (p. 26). While purely social programming can have its place in postsecondary education, it does not always have a positive effect on student success for Black male collegians (see Wood, 2012a), nor is it necessarily a core responsibility of the institution. Rather, academic and co-curricular programs that provide Black men with opportunities to engage in research experiences, academically-oriented clubs and organizations (Harper, 2010), study abroad, community service (Harris et al., 2010), and learning communities (Wood & Hilton, 2012) should be readily available and must target involvement among Black men. This programming is essential to Black male success, as it allows them to engage in educationally purposive activities that reframe and extend upon classroom learning and personal development. Moreover, high-impact practices disproportionately benefit historically underrepresented and underserved students, particularly men of color (Community College Survey of Student Engagement (CCSSE), 2014). Moreover, such programming can also provide students with greater access to networks (social capital) and understanding of the spoken and unspoken structures of academe (cultural capital). Given this, institutional leaders are responsible for ensuring that Black men are represented in high-impact programs, not just those serving remedial needs. This is the litmus test for efficacious practice; not simply having programming in place, but actual use of these programs by Black men.

Table 4.1 Eight Key Domains of Institutional Responsibility

Key domains	Select sub-domains	Key responsibilities
Programs	• Academic • Co-curricular	• Engagement • Socio-cultural capital
Policies	• Institutional • Inter-institutional • Regional/statewide • Federal	• Racial parity • Resource equity • Accountability
Practices	• Student services • Teaching and learning • Strategic planning • Hiring, retention, advancement • Professional growth	• Intrusive • Culturally relevant • Strategic • Collaborative • Equitable
Resources	• Students • Programs and services • Strategic initiatives	• Building capacity • Sustaining advancements
Structures	• Physical structure • Compositional structure	• Belonging • Access • Proportionality
Climates	• Organizational psyche • Normative communication • Normative beliefs • Normative actions	• Critical agency • Affirmation • Anti-racism • Dialogue
Partnerships	• PreK-12 • Postsecondary education • Industry	• College preparedness • Fluid transitions • Professional opportunities
Inquiry	• Students • College personnel • Programs and services	• Culture of critical analysis • Onus for outcomes • Learning organization

The second domain of institutional responsibility is *policy*. Policy is an essential element of consideration given that it often serves as the backbone of institutional practices, functions, and activities. Much of the policy focus relevant to meeting the needs of Black men are academic policies (e.g., add/drop, withdrawal, filing deadlines) and services (e.g., work study, institutional aid) that seem to have an adverse impact on these men. As such, colleges and universities have a responsibility to enact institutional policies that foster student success, not inhibit it. From a CRT perspective, policies (e.g., rules, regulations, codes) are created by the powerful to maintain and extend their power. Therefore, extant policy often results in injustice and inequity (Solórzano & Ornelas, 2002; Solórzano & Villalpando, 1998). For example, an institution seeking to increase their rankings will often revise their admission policies to require higher levels of precollege academic preparation (e.g., GPA, SAT scores, ACT scores, AP coursework). Undoubtedly, such policies will benefit students and families who have greater access to resources (e.g., SAT preparation courses, private tutors), attend more affluent schools, and understand how to access advanced coursework (e.g., International Baccalaureate, AP, dual college credit).

Typically, such policies will then disadvantage historically underrepresented and underserved communities, particularly Black communities. As a result, college leaders are responsible for establishing institutional policies that produce racial parity and resource equity. The term, resource equity, is used intentionally here to refer to policies that institutionalize the critical distribution (and redistribution) of resources to programs (e.g., TRIO, summer bridge, first year experience, learning communities) serving the most disadvantaged students. Institutional leaders also have a responsibility for policy advocacy at the inter-institutional, regional/statewide, and federal levels that bolster racial parity and resource equity but also extend accountability for student outcomes. For instance, college leaders must advocate state and federal policies that enhance resources to institutions, specifically for programming geared towards undeserved students (Wood & Hilton, 2012).

Practice is another central domain of institutional responsibility. Practice involves both the formal and informal operations on campus, relevant to student services, teaching and learning, strategic planning, hiring, retention and advancement of personnel, and professional growth (among others). Student services (e.g., academic advising, career counseling, tutoring, financial aid) are needed that mitigate external environmental pressures and support learning. Given that men of color may be reluctant to engage services due to avoidance of help-seeking behaviors (Harris & Harper, 2008; Palmer et al., 2009), intrusive advising and counseling (bolstered by early alert systems) must be enacted and used (Wood & Hilton, 2012). Moreover, research on Black men in college suggests that intrusivity in the classroom is also needed; where faculty members are authentically friendly and caring from the onset, proactively monitor student progress, are attentive to student concerns, and provide regular validation (Wood & Turner, 2011). These are particularly important actions for Black men, as they are typically apprehensive about engaging in the classroom due to their awareness of stereotypical views of them as being academically inferior and unintelligent (Wood, 2014). In addition to classroom intrusivity, the teaching and learning enterprise must also be undergirded by engaging pedagogical practices (Harper, 2010) via culturally relevant pedagogy (Bush, 2004; Pope, 2006). Culturally relevant pedagogy is needed in order to aid students in making real-world connections with course content that has applicability to their socio-cultural realities.

In terms of the meta-level direction of the institutional practice, strategic planning is necessary to provide a framework for continuous improvement. As such, strategic planning is integral to enhancing Black male success in college (Harper, 2006). Most institutions of higher education have strategic plans. Strategic planning processes should target outcomes for historically under-represented students and serve as an institutional guidepost for achieving stated outcomes. Institutions are responsible for ensuring that elements of this plan are then imbedded in services, programs, initiatives, and processes to ensure the success of Black men. Strategic plans to improve Black male success (like all strategic plans) should be constructed collaboratively through genuine dialogue (Harper, 2009), key in on knowledge sharing (Kezar, 2005a; 2005b), and make allowance for informed experimentation of practices (Garvin, 1994). Inevitably, diversification of campus personnel should be one component of any strategic plan for long-term support of Black men. Information derived from organizational learning processes should be used to inform new hiring and orientation procedures to ensure that new and diverse personnel are brought into the organization that can support the strategic plan. In doing so, equity will emerge in hiring, retention, and advancement processes as a key responsibility for institutional leaders. Moreover, a core practice consideration for improving Black male success is professional development (Wood & Hilton, 2012). Institutions are responsible for ensuring that professional development activities are in place and used by campus personnel. To improve outcomes for underserved students, professional development must focus on awareness of racialized practices and differential consequences (i.e., in the application of policy and practice) for people of color (Bensimon, 2005). Specific to Black men, professional development must focus on illuminating differential outcomes, highlighting institutional responsibility for inequities, and creating awareness of practices that foster inequity (e.g., micro-aggressions, stereotypes of Black men, messages regarding men and masculinities).

Resources is the next key domain of institutional responsibility. Resources refer to the financial, intellectual, and human capital assets at the disposal of the institution. All domains examined within this chapter have intersections with resource responsibilities. There are numerous sub-domains where resource responsibilities are evident; these include resources for students (e.g., institutional aid, work study, conference attendance), programs and services, and key initiatives. College leaders should strategically allocate resources to these sub-domains to enhance outcomes for all students, including Black men. Leaders concerned with outcomes for men of color should ensure that resources allocated build institutional capacity (Harris et al., 2010). A true marker on institutional commitment in a given area is the degree to which that area is resourced. In reality, many initiatives designed to improve outcomes for Black men are chronically under-resourced and therefore cannot impact student success. Improving outcomes for any underserved student population should be a core responsibility for all college personnel, not simply another 'task' for one or two

61

individuals. Sustainability is essential, as many efforts to improve outcomes for men of color are not sustainable since they rely upon one-time funds, intermittent funding, and staff with responsibilities in multiple areas (Wood, 2011). While capacity is building, institutions are also responsible for sustaining advancements as supported by institutionalization of dedicated resources. Resources should also be allocated to ensure that appropriate assessment and inquiry are occurring throughout the institution (Dowd, Pak, & Bensimon, 2013). This will increase the likelihood that already limited resources are maximized and being effectively used to redress critical areas of concern.

Institutions also have accountability for their *structures*—both their physical structure and their compositional structure. The physical structure refers to the physical characteristics of institutions, such as their class sizes, office locations, and images. Compositional structures refer to the composition and distribution of their administration, faculty, staff, and students. In terms of the prior—physical structures—colleges and universities should be designed in a manner that fosters interactions among faculty, staff, and students. For instance, the location of faculty office and key resources (e.g., multicultural center, financial aid, advising, tutoring) should encourage interactions for all students. Further, though not specific to Black men, one of the most salient critiques of the physical structure of an institution for students of color comes from Turner (1994) in her article, "Guests in someone else's house." Her research, based on interviews with students of color attending a predominantly White research institution, found that they felt like unwelcomed guests at their own institution. She stated,

> Like students of color in the university climate, guests have no history in the house they occupy. There are no photographs on the wall that reflect their image. Their paraphernalia, paintings, scents, and sounds do not appear in the house. There are many barriers for students who constantly occupy a guest status that keep them from doing their best work.
>
> (p. 356)

In total, she noted that institutions with these physical structures (as well as isolation social structures) prevented students from establishing a sense of belonging, and therefore solidified their isolated status as the 'other' or the 'guest.' As with the students in Turner's research, Black men often occupy a guest status on college and university campuses. Too often, their histories, art, and culture are not represented through images (e.g., pictures, paintings, statutes), thereby constraining them from developing a sense of belonging. Given this, institutional leaders are accountable for ensuring that the physical structures of their institutions are attuned to the diverse needs of the study body.

With respect to the compositional structure of colleges and universities, leaders are responsible for ensuring that access to the institution for students is equitable (Harris et al., 2010) and proportionally reflective of the communities, regions, and states served. For Black men, Harper (2006) sets a higher standard for proportional representation for Black men. Proportional representation is the relative percentage comparison between students, faculty, staff, and administration in comparison to a reference population (Wood, 2008). Harper (2006) contends that an adequate reference population for Black men is athletic teams. Typically, while Black men are underrepresented throughout colleges and universities, they are overrepresented in revenue generating sports (e.g., basketball, football). Therefore, he suggests that the percentage of Black men in college should be proportional to the percentage of these men in sports. Four-year colleges and universities expend extensive resources to ensure that high-quality Black male athletes attend their institutions; the same level of intensity should be directed to recruiting and retaining high-achieving athletic and non-athletic Black men. Beyond the student body, colleges are also responsible for ensuring that proportionality is achieved with personnel who are intellectually (Kezar, 2005b) and ethnically diverse.

Colleges should be committed to hiring, retaining, and advancing Black male personnel (e.g., faculty, staff, administration) (Harper, 2006). For example, prior research has shown that diverse faculty benefit students of color by serving as role models and mentors to them and creating an affirming campus climate (Nevarez & Wood, 2010). This is a particularly important point given that research on Black men has suggested that they are more likely to be engaged by grounds keepers, maintenance technicians, and food service workers, who they report as the primary group of campus personnel from whom they receive encouragement and validation. In contrast, they noted that they have fewer interactions with faculty members, as faculty avoid interactions with them. The key difference between these campus personnel is that the prior group (e.g., grounds keepers, maintenance crew, service workers) were more likely to reflect their same race or racial/gender background than faculty members (Wood, 2010; 2014). However, colleges should not hire personnel of color simply for their ethnic backgrounds. The compositional structure of the college should be replete with personnel and potential hires from all racial/ethnic and gender groups that illustrate a high degree of cultural competency and prior success with diverse students. In other words, colleges should be wary of hiring a faculty member who responds to questions about their ability to teach ethnically diverse populations by stating that "I treat everyone the same, regardless of their background." Instead, individuals who are attentive to differential socio-cultural experiences based on student characteristics are needed to advance outcomes for all students. Ultimately, the compositional structure of the institution should be a tool to foster belonging and affirmation.

Arguably the most core aspect of institutional responsibility is the campus *climate*. The campus climate refers to the day-to-day dispositions (e.g., affective

63

response, self-concept), thinking, and self-perceptions held within the college or university. We see the climate as being manifested in four primary sub-domains, including the organizational psyche as well as normative communications, beliefs, and actions. The organizational psyche refers to the general assumptions and mores held throughout the institution. To improve outcomes for underserved students (as a whole) critical consciousness is needed within the institution (Dowd et al., 2013). That is, organizations should be conscious of their typical practices and beliefs, and be critical about how the 'status quo' or 'business as usual' can lead to exclusion, isolation, and marginality. Instead, the organization must have a 'sense of urgency' about improving outcomes for Black men. This urgency is demarcated by placing a high institutional priority on addressing institutional programs, policies, and practices that subjugate these men (Harper, 2009).

Moreover, the organization must also embrace an internal locus of control, where the institution recognizes its ability to control the academic futures and outcomes of Black men (Harris et al., 2010). This is juxtaposed with traditional external locus of control, where the students, their precollege experiences, and external pressures (e.g., family commitments, work obligations, life stress) have primary control over their academic matters. This point is key; an organizational internal locus of control is essential, as it is a critical ingredient for colleges and universities to improve outcomes for Black male students. In tandem, organizations that are guided by critical consciousness, place high institutional priority on Black male success, and assume the power to improve outcomes for these men, will have the critical agency to do so.

Institutions also bear responsibility for the confluence of normative communication, beliefs, and actions that shape the institutional climate for Black men. By normative, we are referring to the typical modes of operation and messaging that permeate the campus climate. Organizational leaders are responsible for providing campus climates that are authentically affirming, welcoming, non-isolating, and validating (Harper, 2010; Harris et al., 2010). Moreover, the utility of college as a tool for achieving desired life outcomes must be reinforced (Wood & Hilton, 2012). Such climates occur when there is perceived and real support from faculty and peers, and when there are high expectations for Black males as well as for those serving them (Harper, 2009). Institutions are also responsible for providing educational environments for Black men that are anti-racist and color conscious (Bensimon, 2005). Anti-racism involves vigorous exposure of false assumptions and mores as well as progressive action to eradicate racism. For instance, awareness of and response to racial and gender micro-aggressions (Harris et al., 2010) and White privilege (Bensimon, 2005) is needed. The aforementioned affirming and anti-racist environments can only occur when intergroup dialogue and open communication are fostered (Harper, 2009; Kezar, 2005a, 2005b) among key stakeholders (e.g., administrators, faculty, staff, students).

Colleges and universities also have institutional responsibility for strategic *partnerships* with PreK-12, other postsecondary institutions, and industry. With respect to PreK-12 education, colleges are responsible for making students aware of assumed expectations and competencies for collegiate enrollment and success (Wood & Hilton, 2012). Partnerships with local school districts are necessary to ensure that students are being socialized early on for college preparedness and success. This requires programming and services that bring future students 'to the ivory tower' (e.g., community events, academic summer camps, college tours) as well as bringing the 'ivory tower to them' (e.g., outreach, off-site dual credit opportunities). Partnerships with PreK-12 should include, as a core strategy, the involvement of diverse student representatives who can serve as visual role models to show students that college is for them. This can be particularly important for men of color who are oftentimes socialized in prior schooling to perceive school as a White female domain (due to the predominance of White female teachers in PreK-12) (Harris & Harper, 2008). Specifically, Harris and Harper (2008) suggest that the compositional structure of personnel in PreK-12 has inculcated perceptions that school is not for students of color, nor men. Therefore, when a Black student engages in school, they are often perceived as 'acting White' or countering their racial identity. Similarly, when boys engage in school, they may be teased by peers for being a wuss or sissy. The confluence of both of the racial and gender identities for Black males further intensifies these messages (Harris & Wood, in press). Given the aforementioned, colleges and universities are responsible for disrupting erroneous messages about identity and school.

In addition to partnerships with PreK-12, colleges and universities are also responsible for partnerships with other postsecondary institutions. This is a particularly salient recommendation for community colleges. Community colleges serve as the primary pathway into postsecondary education for men of color. Moreover, Black men often enter the community college with the intent to transfer to a four-year college or university (Wood & Palmer, 2014). As noted by several scholars, successful transfer is the result of strong partnerships, articulation agreements, and mutual commitments between both sending and receiving institutions (Jain, Herrera, Bernal, & Solórzano, 2011; Turner, 1988, 1990, 1992; Turner & Fryer, 1990). Thus, sending and receiving institutions must take responsibility for fluid transitions between institutions that foster success. Finally, partnerships with industry are also key to Black male success. In particular, colleges should establish partnerships that result in professional opportunities (e.g., internships, practicum, fellowships, work experiences) that allow graduates to better position themselves for the job market. For example, research on Black male collegians has shown that they are often concentrated in physically demanding jobs, work late night hours, and have jobs that are temporary in nature (Wood, 2010; Wood & Jones, in press). Such experiences are not preparing these men for careers after graduation. Given that Black men face deleterious unemployment rates (even for those who are college educated), this responsibility should be taken seriously.

Manifesting changes in all of the previously described domains requires an institutional commitment to *inquiry*. Colleges must embrace a culture that critically evaluates student outcomes, college personnel, as well as institutional programs and services. The by-products of this should be a culture of critical analysis of experiences, perceptions, and outcomes; onus for disparate outcomes; and a learning organization. Scholars have often used the lens of organizational learning as a framework for understanding how colleges should collect, learn from, and utilize data to improve organizational decision-making (Bensimon, 2005; Dowd et al., 2013; Kezar, 2005a, 2005b). This theory assumes that organizations, just as individuals, can learn and change over time. Bensimon (2005) noted that learning organizations uncover the role of institutional actors (via their mores, practices, beliefs, expectations) in fostering inequitable outcomes for students. Garvin (1994) suggests that organizational learning is a systematic problem-solving process whereby the scientific method and statistical tools are used to remove assumption, 'gut facts,' and 'sloppy reasoning' from quality improvement efforts (p. 21). Kezar (2005b) extends upon this purely cognitive lens, suggesting that organizational learning also has an affective component as well, where critical thinking is also undergirded by sentiment, ingenuity, and intuition.

Harper and Kuykendall (2012) noted that initiatives and efforts designed to enhance outcomes for Black men must also rely upon inquiry via data-driven decision-making. This will ensure that interventions are informed but also subject to testing for efficacy. In inculcating a culture of inquiry, college leaders must engage in critical analysis of data that are disaggregated to reflect outcomes for historically underrepresented and underserved students. More importantly, when disaggregated data illuminate disparities, leaders should then engage in inquiry to determine how these disparities are manifested by the institution (Bensimon, 2005). For instance, this could include analysis of Black male student out-comes data (e.g., achievement, transfer, attainment, honors participation, post-baccalaureate experiences, participation in high impact practices) (Harris et al., 2010), then be followed up with evaluations of campus services, faculty pedagogy, and following-up with men to determine how the college contributed to them dropping out (Wood & Hilton, 2012).

Disaggregated data and results from inquiry cannot stay within a small cadre of leaders; the data must be transparent to all institutional personnel (Harper & Kuykendall, 2012). Data transparency is essential, as all individuals within the organization should be aware of disparities. Simply put, it is very difficult for organizational affiliates to become advocates for equity when they do not understand the inequitable differences that they have fostered. The literature on

66

organizational learning places strong emphasis on collaborative inquiry teams (Kezar, 2005a, 2005b) that employ practitioner-based models (Harris et al., 2010). As a result, inquiry is not solely a responsibility of researchers (e.g., faculty, institutional research personnel) but of all members within the organization. This is a critical aspect of any learning organization, as individuals may be more likely to respond to findings that they generate from their data, as opposed to results presented to them by 'others.' Collaborative practitioner teams should also engage in reflective practice (Dowd et al., 2013), where key stakeholders reflect upon their role in fostering the outcomes that they have produced.

CONCLUDING REMARKS

The totality of the eight domains of institutional responsibility (e.g., programs, policies, practices, resources, structures, climates, partnerships, inquiry) work to produce positive student outcomes. The benefit of these domains as embodied within the CAO model is the proper specification of a historically mis-specified model of student success. This revised orientation resituates the burden of student success on organizations, not individual students. To provide clarity on how to enact this model in the areas of research, policy, and practice, the next chapter articulates strategies that are necessary for a focus on institutional responsibility.

Chapter 5

Using the CAO Model to Guide Institutional Responsibility Research on Black Men

Black men's dismal college enrollments, disengagement and underachievement, and low rates of baccalaureate degree completion are among the most pressing and complex issues in American higher education. Perhaps more troubling than the problems themselves is the way they are continually mishandled by educators, policymakers, and concerned others. Amplifying the troubled status of Black male students at all levels of education has, unfortunately, yielded few solutions. Thus, educational outcomes for this population have remained stagnant or worsened in recent years. This is attributable, at least in part, to the deficit orientation that is constantly reinforced in media, academic research journals, and educational practice.

(Harper, 2012 p. 1)

Institutional change is a natural outgrowth of institutional responsibility for Black male success. However, as noted by Harper (2012), shifting the burden of collegiate success to the student via a deficit orientation will not produce desirable results. While research and practice focused on improving outcomes for Black men has been spurred by authentic intentionality for advancement, we concur with Harper (2012, 2014) that the deficit orientation has inhibited progress. Specifically, we point to the frameworks of old (e.g., Astin, 1984, 1993; Kuh, 1987; Tinto, 1975) that have shaped the epistemological and philosophical orientation of scholarship and practice as contributing causes for disparate outcomes.

These research paradigms have led to flawed research and interventions because they assumed a locus of causality that begins with the student, not with the institution. Because of this detrimental fallacy, scholars and practitioners have developed questions, designed studies, analyzed data, created interventions, initiated programs, and revised services underpinned by foundational misconceptions. As a result, after decades of mis-specification, colleges and universities still do not adequately serve the lion's share of Black men. As noted by Harper (2014) despite the last 15 years of research and action around Black men, their plight in education has only worsened. We believe this is due to a philosophical foundation that is frail. Guided by the CAO model in the previous chapter, this chapter articulates core elements of research and practice focused on institutional responsibility.

TOWARDS A FIRM FOUNDATION

The importance of a firm foundation cannot be understated. The biblical allegory of a house built on sand versus a house built on rock illustrates the importance of a proper foundation. The house built on sand was supported by a weak foundation, so when tested by the powers of the rain, floods, and wind, the house fell. In contrast, the house built on rock withstood the rains, the floods, and the winds. Despite all the beating withstood, the house did not fall. A conceptualization of factors affecting student success beginning with the student's effort, background, and responsibilities represents the house built on sand (e.g., Astin, 1984, 1993; Kuh, 1987; Tinto, 1975). Despite the ornate walls of scholarship and seemingly firm ceilings of practice erected on this foundation, the house itself remains weak and ineffective. Tested by the rains of contentious organizational governance, the floods of student diversity, and the winds of dwindling institutional resources, the house will fall by fostering stratification and inequity (particularly for Black men). In contrast, a foundation rooted in institutional responsibility and accountability represents the house built on rock. Given the strong foundation, the walls of scholarship and ceilings of practice can withstand the environmental pressures while fostering positive outcomes for students. Unfortunately, much of the scholarship on student success in postsecondary education has been built on a weak foundation. Therefore, the effect of this scholarship on practice has been futile, particularly for historically under-represented and underserved men.

The arrival at this critical point of futility is a function of the interrelationship between epistemology, ontology, and methodology. These elements are all critical components of a paradigm. A paradigm is a philosophy that guides one's view of the world. As noted by Entman (1993) a paradigm is "a general theory that informs most scholarship on the operation and outcomes of any particular system of thought and action" (p. 395). Guba and Lincoln (1994) noted that these paradigms address several primary areas of concern: (a) ontology: "the form and nature of reality and, therefore, what . . . can be known about it" (p. 108); (b) epistemology: "the relationship between the knower or would-be knower and what can be known" (p. 108); and (c) methodology: how "the inquirer (would-be-knower) goes about finding out whatever he or she believes can be known" (p. 108).

Epistemology and ontology shape the core assumptions that undergird methodology. For the 'traditional,' 'status-quo' research on student success, what can be known and the relationship with the known begins with the individual and focuses on their relationship with greater social life. This is likely due to the predominance of sociological disciplinary lenses used in higher education research. Tierney (1992) noted that much of higher education research on student success emanates from the works of Spady (1970) and Tinto (1975, 1993), whose research is clearly sociological. Tierney noted that their work was grounded in the writings of Durkheim, "the father of modern sociology [who] posited that the degree to which an individual was integrated into the fabric of societal institutions lessened the likelihood that someone experienced anomie" (p. 606).

This historical underpinning of the sociological tradition provides insight into how the focus on the student as opposed to the institution began. As a result of this disciplinary orientation, the methodologies employed to examine student success have focused on students' background (e.g., high school GPA, parents' highest level of education, income), academic (e.g., use of services, discussions with faculty, hours spent studying), and social (e.g., friendships on campus, participation in clubs) predictors of integration, involvement, and engagement. Even Bean and Metzner's (1985) model of non-traditional student attrition (which is widely viewed as counter to Tinto's paradigm) has avoided any meaningful focus on institutional factors affecting student success. Bean and Metzner extended the importance of students' external environments and psychological outcomes as core attrition factors, noting that the external lives of students shape their experiences in colleges and can pull them away from academic matters. In attempting to provide a critique of Tinto, Bean and Metzner simply extended the deficit tradition.

In the previous chapter, we articulated the CAO model that is buttressed by the eight domains of institutional responsibility. Here, we highlight key methodological strategies for investigating Black male success for an institutional responsibility research (hereafter referred to as IRR).[1] These elements include: (a) an applied orientation; (b) appropriate theorizing; (c) accounting for student effort; (d) disaggregation of data; (e) focus on the effect of institutional actions; (f) perceptions of the institution; and (g) personal factors as filters. These elements are essential for improving upon prior research.

SEVEN STRATEGIES FOR IRR ON BLACK MALE COLLEGIANS

Applied Orientation

The first aspect of IRR is a dedication to the *applied orientation*. Research designed to improve organizations should be predominantly (though not entirely) applied in nature. By applied, we suggest that this research should be focused on having a direct effect on organizational outcomes (e.g., academic performance, affective development, cognitive development). Research that is most likely to improve desired outcomes will tend to be less theoretical and more interested in how the results will directly and tangibly inform the eight domains of institutional responsibility (i.e., programs, policies, practices, resources, structures, climates, inquiry, partnerships). In contrast, research for the sake of knowledge production with no tangible recommendations for change will not improve the lives of Black men (or other underrepresented groups). This notion of a focus on applied research emanates from a critical race theory perspective dedicated to uncovering inequity, challenging domination, and fostering new systems of power through social justice (Yosso, 2005). Bensimon (2011) suggests that research without an applied orientation is like a physician who examines a patient, theorizes about the problem, but never treats the patient to improve their health. Many would contend that such treatment would be malpractice. Similarly for research on historically underrepresented men (such as Black men), researchers who understand the multiplicity of challenges facing them yet do not provide concrete recommendations for treatment are engaged in negligence. Thus, to improve outcomes for Black men, research should provide concrete recommendations that are accessible to lay audiences that empower them to better serve these men.

Appropriate Theorizing

Appropriate theorizing is the second element of research on Black men focused on institutional responsibility. As noted in Chapter 3, the majority of scholarship on Black men has employed traditional frameworks (e.g., Bandura, 1986; Bean & Metzner, 1985; Tinto, 1975). Moreover, these frameworks have often been developed on populations of White men in four-year colleges and universities. Further, we have argued that these frameworks reify inequity rather than produce parity. Instead, frameworks that have been created specific to the Black male experience are woefully underutilized. In this chapter and in Chapter 4, we illustrate how the traditional frameworks have placed the onus of student success on the student as opposed to the institution. Therefore, future scholarship on Black men should employ frameworks attentive to the unique yet distinctive (non-homogenous) realities of Black men (e.g., African American Male Theory (Bush & Bush, 2013a), Anti-Deficit Achievement Theory (Harper, 2010; 2012), Expressions of Spirituality (Herndon, 2003), Prove-Them-Wrong Syndrome (Moore et al., 2003), and Capital Identity Projection (Wood & Essien-Wood, 2012)) as well as lenses that place the onus of responsibility on the institutions that serve them (e.g., the SEO model (Harris & Wood, in press), Eight Standards of Institutional Efforts for Black Men (Harper & Kuykendall, 2012)). Moreover, we recommend the use of the CAO model to focus directly on institutional actions (e.g., programs, policies, practices, resources, climates, structures) influencing outcomes for these men.

Controlling for Student Effort

The third core element for institutional responsibility research on Black men is *controlling for student effort*. Typically, student effort has been measured via time-spending patterns (e.g., time spent studying, preparing for class, completing assignments), active learning (e.g., asking questions in class, making class presentations, preparing multiple drafts of papers, completing readings on time) and action control (i.e., measures of students' focus on school, work ethic, and drive). When used as independent variables and/or predictors of desired outcomes (e.g., engagement, achievement, persistence), these variables simply reinforce a perspective focused on what the student is or is not doing to facilitate their success. Qualitatively, this involves findings themes evident across men whose levels of effort and engagement are varied.

Quantitatively, we contend that the analogous approach is to employ student effort (or related measures) as a control variable instead of using effort as independent or predictor variables. This approach will hold constant the differential effect of student effort and allow the research to hone in on the relationship between institutional predictors (e.g., faculty validation, service efficacy, high impact practices) and student success outcomes. One clear example of this comes from Wood and Ireland (2014) in their research on determinants of faculty–student engagement for Black men in the community college. Their research used active learning as a control variable, and then focused on the effect of institutional program and services (e.g., learning communities, orientation, study skills courses), college climates (e.g., college-level sense of belonging and diversity interactions), and college characteristics (e.g., college size, urbanicity) to examine the role of these factors on fostering environments of engagement. Their research highlighted the benefits of learning communities, study skills, courses, and orientation programming for engagement.

Disaggregation

The fourth key component of effective, institutionally focused research on Black men is *disaggregation*. The overwhelming majority of research on Black men in higher education portrays them as a single group (see critiques by Cuyjet, 2006; Harper, 2004, 2005, 2006; Harper & Quaye, 2007; Strayhorn & Terrell, 2010). This perceptive avoids acknowledgement of their unique backgrounds, interactions, cultural variations, affiliations, and ethnicities (Harper & Nichols, 2008; Palmer & Wood, 2012; Strayhorn, 2013). A growing body of research on

73

Black men has increasingly focused on differential nuances, acknowledging that institutions provide different learning environments that create disparate experiential realities for Black men (Cuyjet, 2006; Harper, 2004; Strayhorn & Terrell, 2010; Wood & Turner, 2011).

Key differences within the Black male population cannot be trivialized. From an institutional responsibility perspective, heterogeneity requires programming, policies, structures, and resources that serve the unique needs of students. For instance, professional development programming to enhance faculty members' ability to adequately serve their students requires an understanding of the distinctiveness across student populations. As a result, disaggregation of Black men by key characteristics and intersections is necessary (Palmer & Wood, 2012). For example, quantitative models that examine the effect of institutions on Black male success should examine how those relationships differ between African Americans, Mixed-Race Blacks, West Africans, East Africans, Afro-Latinos etc. without collapsing them into a single group for analytic purposes. Moreover, intersections of class, ability status, sexual orientation, and other salient identities should be modeled as separate sub-groups, not solely as control variables.

In addition, there are key differences between Black male populations across institutional types (e.g., HBCUs, community colleges, PWIs, MSIs, for-profits). For example, Black men in community colleges (in comparison to their four-year counterparts) are more likely to be older, have children, be married, and to have delayed their enrollment into postsecondary education (Wood, 2013). Given these key differences, there is also a need for further disaggregation by institutional type (Palmer et al., in press; Wood, 2013). We believe that qualitative researchers have been more attuned to these key within-group differences and intersections; however, results are still often presented as salient themes across men, rather than salient themes within men.

A Focus on Institutional Actions

The fifth aspect of IRR is a focus on the effect of *institutional actions*. In the prior chapter, we explicated eight core domains of institutional responsibility, including: programs, policies, practices, resources, structures, climates, inquiry, and partnerships. The core of IRR is an intensive focus on the influence of institutional action in these domains on Black male student success (e.g., persistence, achievement, attainment, transition, labor, market outcomes). In general, IRR should focus on how these eight domains are manifested and enacted. Moreover, this research should emphasize colleges and universities trying to enhance their success in these areas. Harper (2014) extols the importance of this approach, noting that prior research on Black men has tended:

to focus more on fixing the Black male student than on addressing structural and institutional forces that undermined his academic achievement, sense of belonging, and psychosocial development. Teaching him how to survive in racist classroom environments, for example, was often chosen over educating professors about the ways their pedagogical practices and other actions sustained racism and the marginalization of Black men in courses they taught.

(p. 127)

Harper's (2010, 2012) anti-deficit achievement framework presents a compelling repositioning of questioning needed in a new line of research on Black men. He provides examples of how to reframe questions relevant to them. For example, instead of asking "Why are Black male undergraduates so disengaged in campus leadership positions and out-of-class activities?" he recommends asking "What compelled Black male students to pursue leadership and engagement opportunities on their campus?" While Harper provides several examples of anti-deficit framing, he also provides an example of institutional responsibility framing. For instance, as opposed to inquiring "Why are Black male students' grade point averages often the lowest among both sexes and all racial/ethnic groups on many campuses?" he suggests that practitioners instead ask "What resources proved most effective in helping Black male achievers earn GPAs above 3.0 in a variety of majors, including STEM fields?" (p. 68). Following Harper's logic, IRR requires a repositioning of the typical questions and lines of inquiry that frame research. In Table 5.1, we present how research and practice from an institutional responsibility lens can reframe typical lines of inquiry on Black men.

Perceptions of the Institution

A sixth component of IRR research is a focus on *perceptions of the institution*. Researchers should examine how students believe they are viewed by institutional affiliates (e.g., faculty, staff, administration) as well as other students. Their perceptions of others' views of them help to frame the messaging, micro-aggressions, and nuanced dynamics that emanate from the culture of the institution. For instance, research on sense of belonging serves as an example of this recommendation. Strayhorn (2012) defined sense of belonging as: "students' perceived social support on campus, a feeling or sensation of connectedness, the experience of mattering or feeling cared about, accepted, respected, valued by, and important to the group (e.g., campus community) or others on campus (e.g., faculty, peers)" (p. 3).

The ways in which sense of belonging has been measured by scholars differs. For instance, Maestas, Vaquera, and Zehr (2007) measure belonging using students' perceptions of their connectedness to campus. Similarly, other scholars have operationalized belonging as students' perceptions of 'fit' with the institution

Table 5.1 Reframing Practice and Research from an Institutional
Responsibility Lens

Student responsibility framing	Institutional responsibility reframing
	Practice
Why are these guys so unprepared?	• How are we partnering with PreK-12 to ensure Black men are aware of college entrance requirements? • How are we collaborating with high schools to ensure that Black men are participating in dual credit opportunities? • How are we transitioning Black men from remedial services to academic excellence programming?
We have low yield rates, why are they enrolling elsewhere and not here?	• How does our recruitment process impede access for Black men? • How do initial experiences with admissions and financial aid staff deter them from coming here? • How are we using institutional research personnel to identify how our climate is conveying messages that inhibit access?
Why are they so disengaged in campus life?	• How are we purposively engaging Black men in high-impact practices (e.g., research experiences, academic clubs, study abroad)? • How are we remediating our faculty members to better engage Black men through culturally relevant practices? • How can we ensure that our student affairs staff are validating our Black men?
Why don't they care?	• Are faculty creating an environment of belonging that communicates care for Black men? • How do we ensure our faculty are aware of micro-aggressions that they are conveying to Black men? • Are we assessing Black male perceptions of care from our student service staff?
Are they seeking out help when they need it?	• What intrusive services (e.g., mandatory advising, tutoring) are we providing to ensure they get help when they need it? • What kinds of professional development programming do we have in place that help us better serve our male students? • Are we using early alert systems to identify students who may need some extra support?

Table 5.1 continued

Student responsibility framing	Institutional responsibility reframing
	Research
What background characteristics (e.g., age, income, disability) of Black men predict their persistence?	• What institutional practices predict Black male persistence? • How do campus administrators build stakeholder relationships across the institution to better serve Black men? • What are the most integral programs for increasing non-cognitive outcomes (e.g., self-efficacy, locus of control, intrinsic interest) for Black men? • What aspects of college programs, policies, and practices result in differential outcomes for men by the intersections of age, income, disability etc.
How do Black men make meaning of their experience in college?	• How are institutions fostering negative racialized and gendered experiences for Black men? • What messages are being communicated to Black men through the institutions' compositional diversity? • How are institutions fostering social stratification among Black men?
What causes Black men to be resilient?	• What institutional barriers are in place that require Black men to be resilient? • How can colleges and universities empower Black males to succeed? • How do institutions use inquiry (e.g., assessment, evaluation, research) to better understand the effectiveness of their service to Black men?
Are Black men making connections with their faculty members in and out of the classroom?	• Do faculty members make Black men feel comfortable interacting with them in and out of the classroom? • What are effective training programs that can remediate ineffective faculty? • Do faculty members validate Black men? • What proportion of between college variance in student outcomes is explained by validating experiences from faculty?

(Ostrove, 2003; Ostrove & Long, 2007; Ostrove, Stewart, & Curtin, 2011). Somewhat differently, other scholars have measured sense of belonging focusing on students' perspectives of their relationships with students, administration, and faculty (Hoffman, Richmond, Morrow, & Salomone, 2003; Strayhorn, 2008). Both of these approaches lend insight into how the student interprets their own sense of fit.

While important, another approach that refocuses on perceptions of the institution is used by Wood and Harris (2013) in their institutional needs assessment, "The community college survey of men" (CCSM). In this instrument, students reflect about their relationships with a specific faculty member by indicating their level of agreement with the following statements: "faculty care about my perspective in class"; "faculty value interacting with me during class"; "faculty value my presence in class"; "faculty care about my success in class"; and "faculty believe I belong here." This repositioning of the concept of belonging represents respondents' perceptions of institutional affiliates' viewpoints. We believe this sort of repositioning is key to an IRR approach.

Personal Factors as Filters

The seventh component of IRR on Black male collegians is the use of *personal factors as filters*. Much of the student-focused quantitative research on student success takes into account their background/defining characteristics (e.g., age, income, time status, veteran status, primary language, generational status, ability) and intrapersonal factors (e.g., self-efficacy, locus of control, degree utility, action control, intrinsic interest). Moreover, Harris and Harper (2008) and Harper (2014) have recommended that research on Black men be attentive to both their racial and masculine identities. These background/defining, intrapersonal, and identity factors are all core considerations influencing outcomes for Black men in postsecondary education. However, when examined as factors affecting (qualitative) or determinants of (quantitative) outcomes (e.g., achievement, persistence) for Black men, these integral factors refocus the analysis on the student not the institution. That being said, it is clear that research which does not consider these factors, particularly their gendered identities, fails to adequately address the unique experience of Black men. Thus, we recommend that personal factors be viewed as filters for which the institutional experience is interpreted.

For quantitative research, this suggests modeling the effect of institutional actions (e.g., programs, policies, practices, climates) on student outcomes (e.g., academic performance, cognitive development, affective development) using personal factors (e.g., background, intrapersonal factors, identities) as mediating variables. One example of this approach comes from Newman, Wood, and Harris (in press) in a study of factors influencing perceptions of belonging from faculty members for Black men in the community college. In their study, three primary predictor variables (e.g., perceptions of racial-gender stereotypes from faculty, validating experiences from faculty, and faculty–student engagement) were modeled as predictors of perceptions of belonging with masculine identity (e.g., school as a feminine domain, breadwinner orientation, competitive ethos, help-seeking behaviors) and racial identity variables used as interaction terms. Thus, they were able to make statements about the effect of faculty on Black males' perceptions of belonging while still accounting for how these institutional factors are modified via respondents' identities. A similar approach can be taken with cross-level interactions (in multi-level modeling) to examine aggregate measures of institution climate with personal mediators. For qualitative research, a similar approach can be taken, where examinations of perceptions, experiences, and meaning-making from institutional actions (e.g., validation from staff, perceptions of care from staff, campus racial climate) are examined through the lens of intersectionality.

A PROACTIVE RESPONSE TO CRITICISM

Now that we have articulated our perspective on IRR, we would like to take some space here to proactively address two potential critiques of the ideology. Scholars and practitioners alike may perceive this work as 'blaming the institution.' In no way do we suggest that the institution is the root cause of Black male underachievement. Nor are practitioners solely to blame for deleterious outcomes for Black men. To be clear, one (among several) root cause of inadequate actions relevant to Black men originates from researchers and theoreticians. One of the scholarly community's roles is to serve as 'thought leaders' for the academic training of practitioners. Unfortunately for Black males, the core notions undergirding the training of practitioners have been flawed. In turn, practitioners have adhered to the predominant ideologies emanating from their academic training, focusing on students as the locus of causality for achievement as opposed to the institutions that serve them.

Given this context, we concur with Bensimon and Malcom (2012) that rather than being solely focused on 'remediating' the student, there is a need to remediate the faculty and staff that serve them. In this vein, they argued that there is a need to "remediate practices—in admissions and recruitment, in classrooms, in tutoring centers, in science labs, in counseling services—that are failing students of color, and to create new practices where needed" (pp. 3–4). To remediate suggests that in prior training one did not learn (or was not taught) the necessary tools and concepts that were needed. In this case, we contend that practitioners have been improperly trained by thought leaders, of which the root cause is one of epistemological and ontological origin.

Another similar critique that is necessary to address is the role of student responsibility. Some may perceive this volume as being fully avoidant of addressing the students' role in studying, attending class, meeting with faculty, and the execution of other necessary academic habits. Unequivocally, we believe that students are responsible for critical self-agency to improve their own lives. Students have responsibility for their academic outcomes, as such; we do not seek to belittle the self-determination necessary for success. That being said, we perceive the conversation on responsibility as a pendulum, with one end of the continuum representing student responsibility and the other end representing institutional responsibility. For decades, the focus of student responsibility has been so predominant that the pendulum must swing in the other direction toward institutional responsibility.

Specifically, the years of practice relevant to Black men that has focused on student responsibility have produced little in the way of improvement (Harper, 2014). That is because, like all students, Black males are by-products of the environments that they are socialized in. As noted by Marks (2014), "how do we blame [students] for reacting to environments that we create?" In contrast, a student educated in an environment of affirmation, high expectations, and racial parity will succeed. Thus, the focus on institutional responsibility that empowers Black men is needed. Of course, a student attends college for only a few short years. While these colleges and universities cannot be expected to undo the damage that has been caused by the preponderance of their precollege experiences, colleges can and must make strides to better support Black men.

CONCLUDING REMARKS

This chapter has provided a description of seven core elements that are indicative of institutional responsibility research on Black men. These elements include: (a) an applied orientation; (b) appropriate theorizing; (c) accounting for student effort; (d) disaggregation of data; (e) focus on the effect of institutional actions; (f) perceptions of the institution; and (g) personal factors as filters. As expounded upon in this chapter, we believe that prior research and practice on Black men is fundamentally flawed, in that the onus of success rests on students, as opposed to the institutions that serve them. While we do not seek to take away the importance of students' responsibility for their own success, we do envision that Black men will experience enhanced outcomes (e.g., persistence, achievement, attainment) through a remediation of research and practice that has failed to improve their educational realities and outcomes.

NOTE

1   Readers interested in a more specific articulation of ways to improve research on Black men (in general) should see Shaun Harper's (2014) chapter, "(Re)setting the agenda for college men of color: Lessons learned from a 15-year movement to improve Black male student success."

Chapter 6

Strategies for Recruiting and Supporting Black Men in Higher Education

In the prior two chapters, we explicated the CAO model of institutional responsibility for Black male success. We also discussed strategies for using the model to advance research on Black men in postsecondary education. In this chapter, we turn to the use of the model for institutional practice. Herein, we discuss differing strategies for 'Action,' embodied in the CAO model that has direct implications for Black male recruitment, retention, and student affairs programming. Specifically, this chapter provides an in-depth description of practice recommendations based on three 'Action' elements: partnerships, climates, and programs. The three areas are highlighted given that researchers have been more diligent in evaluating strategies in these areas.

CAO: PARTNERSHIPS

The importance of partnerships was identified as a core institutional responsibility in the CAO model. Specifically, partnerships that foster college preparedness and fluid transitions between institutions (e.g., high school to college, community college to university), were extolled. Moreover, given the information discussed in Chapter 2 regarding issues that hinder the academic preparedness of Black males in PreK-12, postsecondary education institutions should focus on establishing a comprehensive alliance with their local PreK-12 school district to help increase preparedness among Black males for higher education. In fact, Howard (2006) noted that the most critical intervention that colleges and universities can implement to increase access and success among Black males is the formation of an educational alliance between PreK-12 and postsecondary education. There are several trends occurring in higher education, which make the implementation of educational alliances between higher education and PreK-12 particularly urgent. First, affirmative action seems to be increasingly facing demise.

The primary purpose of affirmative action is to promote access and equity for underrepresented minorities in programs using federal funds. While higher education has generally used affirmative action to increase access among underrepresented minorities and women (Kaplin & Lee, 2007), it has been challenged in the courts over the years. In fact in the most recent challenge to affirmative action—*Fisher v. University of Texas* (2013)—while the Supreme Court reaffirmed the ability of institutions to use race to diversify their student bodies, some fear that the Court's decision could lay the groundwork for the demise of affirmative action (Barnes, 2013; Carr, 2013).

In addition to the potential demise of affirmative action and its impact on limiting access to higher education for Black students, another trend that increases the necessity of a comprehensive partnership between higher education and PreK-12 is the fact that remedial programs are gradually being dismantled at four-year public institutions. Research has demonstrated that a large number of undergraduate students enroll in remedial courses at four-year colleges (Attewell, Lavin, Domina, & Levey, 2006). Given that 80 percent of Black students leave high school academically underprepared (Kimbrough & Harper, 2006; Davis & Palmer, 2010), they are more likely to rely on college remediation for access to postsecondary education.

In addition to the potential dismantlement of affirmative action and college readiness programs, another trend that highlights the importance for colleges to be more intentional about forming a cohesive partnership with PreK-12 to help increase the academic preparedness of Black males is that funding of TRIO programs continues to be reduced. Congress implemented TRIO programs in the 1960s to help low-income students of color access and succeed in post-secondary education (Swail et al., 2003). Though TRIO programs have been successful in helping facilitate college access and success for students of color, they have sustained budget cuts over the years (Burd, 2011), greatly reducing their efficacy. Given that the existence of the aforementioned initiatives is being threatened and seems to be facing dismantlement, postsecondary educational institutions ought to consider building a comprehensive alliance with their local PreK-12 school system. Doing so would accomplish at least three goals:

1. It would ensure that Black males are well prepared academically.
2. It would increase the extent to which students are familiar with students, educators, and administrators of the institution, increasing their likelihood of attending the institution upon graduation from high school.
3. It would increase their familiarization with actions needed to prepare for college, such as the college application, financial aid, and standardized testing processes.

Some postsecondary educational institutions have implemented such comprehensive partnerships with their local PreK-12 system and it has helped them achieve these goals. These partnerships are emblematic of the institutional responsibility orientation necessary to foster success for Black men. For example, Florida State University (FSU) implemented the Center for Academic Retention and Enhancement (CARE) program in 2000 (Carey, 2008). With this program, FSU reaches out to low-income, first-generation minority students, as early as sixth grade, to provide advice and support through their high schools and college careers. FSU recruits students to participate in this program by talking to guidance counselors and identifying potential candidates from a list of students eligible for the federal free and reduced lunch program. When these students enter the ninth grade, CARE provides summer and after-school programs that help them negotiate the financial aid process, teaches them how to study for the SAT and ACT, and how to complete college applications. As these students near the completion of high school, they can apply to FSU through the CARE program, on the condition that they participate in a summer bridge program that begins the summer before they matriculate into FSU and extends into their first two years of college.

During the summer bridge program, students live together in a residence hall staffed by upperclassmen counselors. Approximately 300 students participate in this program, which uses a comprehensive philosophy to help students succeed at the institution. In addition to ensuring that students are prepared academically for success at FSU and increasing their familiarity with the financial process, CARE also helps students become familiar with the local community by helping them navigate a range of systems, such as public transportation.

When students enter FSU as freshmen they participate in tutoring sessions and are provided with academic advisors who track their progress until graduation (Carey, 2008). CARE also organizes social events and bimonthly seminars on college success. Research shows that CARE students graduate at almost the same rate as non-CARE students (Carey, 2008). Even more noteworthy, since the implementation of CARE, FSU has experienced tremendous growth in the success of its Black students. In fact, Carey indicated that, by 2006, the graduate rate of Black students was at an historic high. Carey explained, "The fact that the CARE program was implemented during the same time period suggests that it played a role in Florida State's success" (p. 4).

Programs of this nature are not exclusive to large, research-oriented PWIs. Other institutions are also initiating programs that assume responsibility for institutional outcomes. For instance, some HBCUs and community colleges have similar programs. Delaware State University (DSU) is planning to begin a dual enrollment program in 2014. While there are no formal admission criteria to participate in this program, it will only be open to high school students interested in science, technology, engineering, and mathematics (STEM). Once students are enrolled in this program, they will be able to transfer a certain amount of their high school credits into DSU. The program is designed to offer students an early college experience. The intent of this program is to help DSU improve academic preparedness among students and increase the number of students entering into its university.

Though not STEM related, Coppin State University (CSU) provides a similar early college experience program through its Coppin Academy, which is a high school situated on the campus of CSU (Coppin Academy High School, n.d.). Similarly, some community colleges and four-year institutions in California are affiliated with the Mathematics Engineering Science Achievement (MESA) program. This program is a National Foundation of Science funded initiative and involves PreK-12 schools, community colleges, and four-year institutions (Starobin, Jackson, & Laanan, 2012). The primary goal of MESA is to help increase the academic and social preparedness of low-income, first-generation minority students' in STEM. To this end, these students will be at an increased likelihood of entering a four-year college and university and successfully navigating a STEM curriculum (Palmer & Dubord, 2013; Starobin et al., 2012).

One of the most interesting aspects of these partnerships that colleges have with PreK-12 schools is that they are implemented across a range of institutional types. Although they may be different in various ways, as illustrated by the aforementioned context, these partnerships cannot only help to increase the academic preparedness of Black males for higher education, but they can also serve as a critical tool for recruitment. As such, we urge institutions to study the programs articulated and give serious consideration to establishing a similar program, if one is not in existence at their institution.

Perhaps institutions may not have the financial resources or human capital to establish a comprehensive partnership with PreK-12 schools in their neighborhood. In such cases, institutions may consider encouraging their upperclassmen to get involved in local schools near the college. In this capacity, students could serve as mentors and tutors to students in general and Black males in particular. This exchange might create opportunities for Black males to learn more about college—academically and socially. Furthermore, the interaction that Black males will have with these upperclassmen may create opportunities for the college students to serve as role models to some of the Black male students. Increasing the accessibility that Black males have with role models is critical because, oftentimes, they lack access with such positive figures (Harper, 2006, 2012; Jackson & Moore, 2006, 2008; Palmer & Maramba, 2011; Strayhorn, 2008). By Black males having access and contact with these upperclassmen, perhaps they will develop a great rapport with the college students, leading them to consider attending college, if they were not already planning to. In fact, this exchange may encourage Black males to attend the college in which the upperclassmen are enrolled.

Another way in which this partnership between local PreK-12 schools and higher education institutions could manifest is through the college sending educational administrators, such as student affairs practitioners, to the school to offer cultural competency workshops to teachers and counselors. In Chapter 2, we noted that teachers and counselors in the PreK-12 systems are more likely to have low expectations for the academic talent and potential of Black students. As such, research has shown that these teachers and counselors are less inclined to encourage Black students to enroll in AP courses and possibly even consider going on to college. Thus, if colleges provided ongoing cultural competency training to these educators in the PreK-12 system, perhaps they would think more highly of Black students in general and their potential to succeed in college specifically. If this were to happen, it may result not only in more Black students participating in AP courses, but also it may increase the number of Black students pondering going on to higher education, which would increase the pool of Black students that institutions could recruit to their campuses.

In addition to establishing a partnership with local PreK-12 schools, which may encourage more students in general and Black males specifically to enroll in that institution, colleges should also consider being proactive to raise funds to help support students as they matriculate into higher education. Previously, we indicated that one of the critical elements that serves as a threat to the access and success of students is the ability to finance their college education. Financing college has worsened over the years, as tuition has steadily increased while state support for higher education and merit aid has declined. Thus, students are forced to rely more on loans to help finance their college education (General Accounting Office, 1995). Since Black students tend to be averse to loans (Swail et al., 2003), many Black males may be more likely to work off campus to ensure that they have the financial resources to help support their education (Palmer et al., 2009).

Given this, colleges and universities should engage in fundraising initiatives to help support Black males as well as other students in need. We know that some HBCUs and many PWIs have implemented fundraising campaigns. At these institutions, these campaigns have taken the form of faculty and staff giving initiatives. Similarly, these campaigns have also involved working to actively engage alumni so that they are willing to give financially to help support current students who are struggling financially. While these recommendations may seem fairly simplistic, some institutions have not fully embraced the power of creating fundraising initiatives (Gasman & Bowman, 2011). For example, though Morgan State University (MSU) now has these fundraising initiatives, they are relatively new to this practice. MSU's efforts are timely because since the U. S. Department of Education changed the eligibility requirement for the Parent PLUS Loan, a number of students at HBCUs have been forced to 'stop out' because of lack of financial resources (Doubleday, 2013).

Colleges and universities should also work with current minority students and alumni to help recruit and identify prospective Black male applicants. Indeed, each student who comes to college has a network of other students who may be of the same race and may be qualified for admission. Furthermore, four-year colleges and universities should consider establishing transfer programs with community colleges. This can assist in creating a pipeline of qualified Black male applicants. As discussed in Chapter 1, a large percentage of Black males begin their postsecondary education experience at community college. Naturally, this situates community colleges as a primary door to help four-year colleges and universities increase the number of Black males on their campuses. Given that this chapter has provided a number of initiatives that institutions could do to increase Black male enrollment on their campuses, the subsequent section of this chapter will summarize those strategies below.

Table 6.1 Summary of Strategies to Increase Colleges and Universities'
Efforts to Recruit Black Males

Steps	Description of Interrelated Strategies
1	Colleges and universities should establish a comprehensive alliance with local PreK-12 schools. In addition to helping facilitate academic preparedness among Black males, it may encourage them to attend that institution because they will be familiar with faculty, staff, and administrators.
2	Encourage upperclassmen to serve as mentors and tutors to Black male students in nearby schools. Not only will this create opportunities for the upperclassmen to serve as role models for these students, but this interaction may encourage Black males to enroll into the educational institution that their tutor or mentor attends.
3	Encourage faculty and student affairs practitioners to provide cultural competency training to local PreK-12 educators. In this vein, PreK-12 educators will think more highly of the academic potential of Black males, which may result in more PreK-12 educators encouraging more Black males to enroll in AP courses or consider attending college. With this approach, it will create a larger pool of Black males for colleges and universities to recruit to their campuses.
4	Provide scholarships to students in general and Black males specifically in financial need as they matriculate into the institution. This may prove difficult to certain institutions, such as community colleges and some HBCUs.
5	Colleges and universities should work with current minority students or alumni to help identify prospective Black male applicants.
6	Four-year colleges and universities should form better partnerships with community colleges to help increase the number of Black males on campus.

CAO: CLIMATES

A core institutional responsibility identified in the 'Action' domain of the CAO model is the creating institutional climates that foster affirmation and critical agency. As evident in the graphical depiction of the CAO model (presented in Chapter 5), climates are directly influenced by institutional structures, programs, policies, and practices. One integral method for achieving this end is through validation. Rendón's (1994) theory of validation emphasizes the importance of in-class as well as out-of-class institutional agents engaging in activities that support, enable, or confirm students' skills and abilities, leading to academic and interpersonal development. Given the chilly campus climate that students of color encounter at PWIs (see Chapter 1), the CAO model could have important implications for helping college administrators at PWIs better support Black men.

According to Chapter 1, research has demonstrated that HBCUs have a positive reputation for making Black students feel like they matter throughout their college experience, including the recruitment stage (Allen, 1992; Davis, 1994; Fries-Britt & Turner, 2002; Gasman, 2008, 2013; Kim & Conrad, 2006; Palmer & Wood, 2012). Research suggests that they do this by creating a family-oriented environment where students feel welcomed and important. Thus, these students may be more inclined to enroll in HBCUs because administrators and faculty with whom they had a chance to interact during the college search phase have impressed upon them that they matter. While this may be the case, similar to other institutional types, HBCUs can certainly work to enhance aspects of their campus ethos (e.g., customer service), to be more intentional about creating an environment where students feel like they matter across all segments of the campus community.

Despite this, there are some important lessons that PWIs and possibly community colleges could learn from HBCUs in terms of helping Black students feel valued as they seek to enroll in higher education. We highlighted these two institutional types because in Chapter 1 research has indicted that Black males tend to perceive administrators and faculty at PWIs and community colleges as unsupportive in regard to helping facilitate their success. With the CAO model in mind, in order to help institutions assume responsibility for Black male access, they should ensure that institutional officials are positive and supportive of students and their validating agents as they first make contact with college and university. They can also do this through practices that demonstrate cultural competence and by showing respect to the concerns that families may have about their son's college experience. While recruiting Black males to colleges and universities is critical, once they enroll in higher education, colleges and universities have to work to keep them enrolled. Consequently, using the CAO model as a guide, we discuss ways that community colleges, HBCUs, and PWIs can attempt to increase retention and persistence among Black male students by providing opportunities of support and validation.

Aside from ensuring that Black male students encounter supportive and caring institutional agents as they make contact with the institution, institutions need to continue to ensure that Black males encounter a positive, validating, anti-racist, and affirming educational environment once they matriculate into college. A climate of support spans what occurs both inside and outside the classroom. One of the strategies that universities can employ is to encourage campus affiliates (e.g., faculty, administrators, staff) to be responsible for the success of students. Research has shown that this type of collectivist mindset exists on HBCU campuses (Fleming, 1984; Gasman, 2008, 2013; Fries-Britt & Turner, 2002; Palmer & Gasman, 2008). In fact, Palmer and Gasman reported findings from a qualitative study that investigated factors of success for Black men who entered an HBCU academically underprepared and persisted to graduation. According to Palmer and Gasman, one of the critical factors that played a significant role in the success of these students was that everyone in the institutional community worked to support their success. For example, not only did faculty and administrators go above and beyond their official responsibilities to support the success of the students, but also like-minded peers played a vital role in the retention and persistence of these students. Indeed, these institutional officials supported, encouraged, and validated the Black males inside as well as outside of the classroom.

Research has noted that many key institutional agents at HBCUs help to create a rich environment replete with social capital. This capital helps to facilitate the success of Black males and to create an environment where they feel validated. This is an essential component of the HBCU climate; unfortunately, Black men at other institutional types (e.g., community colleges, PWIs) are often not always afforded the same level of support and validation from institutional agents (Bush & Bush, 2010; Davis, 1994; Feagin et al., 1996; Fries-Britt & Turner, 2002; Guiffrida, 2005; Wood, 2012a–c; Wood & Turner, 2011). For example, as noted in Chapter 1, Black males perceive faculty at PWIs and community colleges as unsupportive and culturally insensitive. To this end, PWIs and community colleges need to work to be more intentional to ensure that Black males receive support and validation from faculty as well as other institutional agents as they matriculate into these institutional contexts. In order to help facilitate this process, college officials should hold workshops on validation, racial/gender micro-aggressions, and culturally relevant practices. Altogether, the influence of these factors on creating a sense of belonging as well as helping to foster academic success should be discussed.

College administrators should also encourage faculty to form partnerships with student affairs officials so they can offer insight into how faculty might integrate validation strategies into their pedagogical activities. Specifically, student affairs practitioners at research-oriented PWIs might need to work with faculty to create a sense of 'buy in' about the importance of validating students in their classroom. While faculty at these types of institutions may recognize the benefit of validating students outside the classroom, some may view this as being outside of their professional purview. To this end, they may be less inclined to do it in the classroom. Wood and Harris's (2013) instrument, the "community college survey of men," provides concrete examples of validating messages that should be communicated from faculty to students. They include professors regularly telling students that they "have the ability to do the work," "they can succeed in college," and "they belong at this institution." Given the negative experiences and interactions that Black males have with faculty at PWIs and community colleges, officials at these institutions should mandate that faculty attend cultural awareness workshops to help them become more informed of how to work with students who differ from them racially, ethnically, and culturally. These workshops should take place on a frequent basis and their occurrence should be codified in institutional policy. Implementing these workshops and encouraging faculty as well as other institutional agents (e.g., staff, administration) to attend them sends a strong message to minority students that the institution values inclusiveness and wants to promote an environment where all students feel a sense of belonging. Further, promulgating these steps would increase the goal of all faculty bearing responsibility for supporting and validating students.

Similarly, in order to further ensure that the institutional environments of PWIs and community colleges are prepared to fully support and validate Black males, PWIs and community colleges should also administer climate surveys to the campus community to have a better understanding of how various constituents of the campus community perceive the campus. If used appropriately, a survey of this nature is useful to help institutions design forums and other workshops about racial micro-aggressions and other issues that engender an uncomfortable campus climate. Furthermore, administrators at these institutions might also consider hiring additional faculty of color and administrators. Doing so is critical because these individuals may serve as an additional form of support for Black men (though the responsibility of supporting students should not fall solely on faculty and administrators of color). This suggestion indicates the interrelatedness of the institution's structural composition (as embodied in the CAO model) with that of the campus climate. We argue that the structural composition of the institutional setting communicates belonging to students of color. Moreover, research has shown that with the presence of more minority faculty and administrators on campus, the prejudice and stereotypical views that White professors, administrators, and students have of students of color may be challenged (Alexander & Moore, 2008; Moody, 2012), hopefully, resulting in more equitable treatment and support for Black male students.

In addition to the aforementioned factors, college administrators at PWIs and community colleges should encourage faculty to be more intentional about establishing rapport and building critical relationships with students. Again, doing this would be critical as it would provide another way for institutions to help support and validate students, particularly Black males. One way to encourage relationship building between faculty and students is to provide opportunities for them to interact outside the classroom. Perhaps if faculty interacted more with students outside of class, they would get to know their students better, thus creating meaningful opportunities for faculty to discard cultural stereotypes they may have about Black males and other minority students. Given that this may be difficulty for students in community colleges because research has indicated that they may have more external commitments than students attending four-year institutions (Mason, 1998; Wood, 2011, 2012a–c), faculty in community colleges may have to be more intentional about using class time and space as a critical opportunity to foster meaningful relationships with students.

CAO: Programs

Another core element of the CAO model is programming that is supportive of Black male achievement. Specifically, programs should employ high-impact practices to support the socio-cultural capital development of Black men. One way that institutions can support and create opportunities to support the academic and psychosocial development of Black males is through mentoring. While research has indicated that Black males who attend HBCUs can readily find a mentor on campus (albeit some research has questioned this—see Chapter 1), research on Black students at PWIs has shown that outside of a few Black faculty and administrators on campus, Black males have challenges finding a mentor on campus. Though research has not thoroughly discussed Black male community college students' accessibility to mentors, given that they perceive faculty as unsupportive, they may face similar challenges to finding a mentor on campus as their counterparts at PWIs. Nevertheless, colleges and universities should encourage and be proactive in linking Black men, particularly those who are first generation, with a mentor. These mentors may be faculty, staff, administrators, alumni, or community members. College administrators should also be mindful that peer mentors can provide important guidance and support to Black men in postsecondary education. Black men, making the initial transition into college, may be able to relate more effectively to successful upperclassmen serving as peer mentors. Not only can peer mentors help to facilitate students' academic and social integration, but also they can share experiences of triumphs and struggles, and expose students to critical resources—academic and social— to help enrich their college experience. As noted previously in the volume, mentorship can be a key strategy for success; however, this is only likely to occur when the matching process is thoughtful, allows for an organic development of mentor–protégé relationships, and is purposeful in nature (i.e., focusing on academic- and career-related activities).

90

Aside from using mentors as a critical way to help support Black male collegians, institutions should continue to establish Black male initiatives (BMIs). Research has indicated that many diverse institutional types (e.g., community colleges, PWIs, HBCUs) have BMIs (see Chapter 2). BMIs play a significant role in helping to facilitate Black male success by helping them establish meaningful relationships with faculty, staff, administrators, and peers. According to Wood and Palmer (2012), effective BMIs are research-based in that program development and implementation are informed by extant research and theory. Specifically, Wood and Palmer explained that BMIs that have a meaningful impact of student success are developed with research on academic and social integration, student engagement, and function to create a welcoming and affirming campus environment. They also noted that successful BMIs have a focus on collectivity, as exemplified through program slogans, mottos, and themes. This suggests that successes and failures are mutually shared. Under this value, collaboration, community, otherness, and equity are important virtues. Third, they opined that program assessment and evaluation were integrated into most programs examined. This allowed for program officials to better understand the impact their programs had on the students served and for enhanced partnerships.

Furthermore, Palmer and Wood (2012) indicated that effective BMIs function to help facilitate students' critical reflection of their personal, academic, and professional goals and philosophical outlook on life. These reflections are facilitated by journaling as well as small and large group discussions. Finally, Palmer and Wood noted that successful BMIs use social networking technologies (e.g., Facebook, Twitter, LinkedIn) to facilitate recruitment, networking, and communication among participants. Interestingly, Wood and Palmer (2012) noted that many institutions with BMIs do not place emphasis on assessing the efficacy of these initiatives. Specifically, they underscored the importance of assessment, indicating that it leads to improvement in core components and services of BMIs, which might enhance the effectiveness of these initiatives. We recognize, as exemplified by the focus on inquiry in the CAO model, that merely having BMIs is not sufficient. In order to truly understand the value of these initiatives and their role in helping support the success of this student demographic, assessing BMIs should be a critical goal for institutions.

One example of a BMI is the Man Up program at Howard University (Wood & Palmer, 2012). Specifically, Man Up was founded in response to poor success rates among Black males at the institution. Man Up is a program that helps to reach beyond the social and classroom problems to help students as they journey through the university and through life. Man Up follows the unofficial theme 'being there for them,' which indicates the program's focus on providing support, encouragement, and resources for male students at Howard. This is accomplished through monthly meetings, which are organized around a group-counseling model. These meetings consist of group discussions, where males sit in a large circle and talk about issues they are confronting in their lives. As part of this initiative, Man Up organizers provide college success and academic-oriented workshops where all students can learn about time management, study skills, and enhance their writing. Aside from these meetings, Man Up staff work with students during discussion sessions to identify their needs. Once identified, staff refer students to workshops and offices most applicable to their needs (Valbrun, 2010). Not only can BMIs help support and validate the academic and psychosocial development of Black male collegians, they can also help encourage campus engagement among this demographic. As discussed in Chapter 2, while engagement on campus has been linked to a variety of outcomes, Black males are generally disengaged across diverse institutional types (Flowers, 2006; Harper & Quaye, 2009; Kimbrough & Harper, 2006; Palmer & Young, 2009; Palmer & Maramba, 2012).

University officials should also consider implementing workshops for Black male students on college success as critical ways to better facilitate and augment the supportive environment that they have established to better support the success of Black male students. Aside from providing critical forms of support, these workshops can also function to help validate the academic and psychosocial development of Black male students. Workshops could cover a variety of topics including (but not limited to): using non-cognitive skills to facilitate student success; awareness of campus resources and services; academic productivity; developing a healthy gender identity; promotion of student involvement in extracurricular activities as well as campus clubs and organizations; and financial planning and financial aid. Given the range of topics needed to both demystify and engage the policies, processes, and procedures of college, college professionals of all positions (e.g., faculty, staff, administrators) could serve as workshop facilitators. Institutions should even consider making certain workshops mandatory in order to ensure that students have received accurate and up-to-date information.

In addition to workshops focused on college success, colleges and universities should implement or expand the number of learning communities on their campuses. Learning communities are a core high-impact practice that is integral to the success of historically underrepresented and underserved students, particularly Black men. Many colleges and universities have learning communities (Visher & Teres, 2011). These communities can be critical sources of support and validation for Black male students. Learning communities are coordinating collections of students who take the same coursework in cohorts. However, a unique attribute of learning communities is that students are grouped around specific background factors. In some cases, learning communities also have residential components, where students co-habit in residence halls and participate in ongoing social programming to facilitate a sense of community (Weiss, Visher, Teres, & Schneider, 2010). Bonner (2012) noted that learning communities foster intellectual and psychosocial development through discourse among groups of collegians around important academic matters and challenges. Further, he noted that these enclaves of students serve as communication networks where information on college life is passed from one student to another. He suggested that practitioners use these communication networks to infuse information needed to ease academic concerns.

CONCLUDING REMARKS

This chapter has presented critical steps that institutions could employ to not only increase the number of Black men on their campuses, but also support them once they enroll into the institution. While the intent of this chapter was to provide important recommendations to help institutional officials better support Black men across diverse institutional types, some recommendations may be more applicable to some institutional types than others. For example, given that Black males are more prone to enroll in community college as opposed to four-year colleges and universities (see Chapter 1), finding ways to recruit Black males to these institutions may not be as salient for community college officials as it might be for officials at other institutional types. The information provided in this chapter can be immensely helpful in helping college administrators, faculty, and student affairs practitioners better facilitate Black male retention and persistence. However, while critical, this information is not meant to be exhaustive, but to provide some fundamental insight into how colleges and universities might work to more effectively recruit Black males to campus and provide a campus environment conducive to their academic success via the CAO model.

References

Alexander, R., & Moore, S. (2008). The benefits, challenges, and strategies of African-American faculty teaching at predominantly White institutions. *Journal of African American Studies*, 12, 4–18.

Allen, W. R. (1986). *Gender and campus race differences in Black student academic performance, racial attitudes and college satisfaction*. Atlanta, GA: Southern Education Foundation.

Allen, W. R. (1992). The color of success: African American college students' outcomes at predominantly White and historically Black public colleges and universities. *Harvard Educational Review*, 62, 26–44.

Allen, W. R., & Jewell, J. O. (2002). A backward glance forward: Past, present and future perspectives on historically Black colleges and universities. *Review of Higher Education*, 25, 241–261.

Aronson, J., Fried, C., & Good, C. (2002). Reducing the effects of stereotype threat on African American college students by shaping theories of intelligence. *Journal of Experimental Social Psychology*, 38, 113–125.

Astin, A. W. (1984). Student involvement: A developmental theory for higher education. *Journal of College Student Personnel*, 25, 297–308.

Astin, A. W. (1993). *What matters in college? Four critical years revisited*. San Francisco, CA: Jossey-Bass.

Attewell, P., Lavin, D., Domina, T., & Levey, T. (2006). New evidence on college remediation. *Journal of Higher Education*, 77, 886–924.

Baber, L. D. (2012). Bicultural experiences of second generation Black American males. In R. T. Palmer & J. L. Wood (Eds.), *Black men in college: Implications for HBCUs and beyond* (pp. 89–106). New York: Routledge.

Bailey, D. F., & Moore, J. L., III. (2004). Emotional isolation, depression, and suicide among African American men: Reasons for concern. In C. Rabin (Ed.), *Linking lives across borders: Gender-sensitive practice in international perspective* (pp. 186–207). Pacific Grove, CA: Brooks/Cole.

Bandura, A. (1986). *Social foundation of thought and action. A social cognitive theory*. Englewood Cliffs, NJ: Prentice-Hall.

Bandura, A. (1995). *Self-efficacy in changing societies*. Cambridge, UK: Cambridge University Press.

Bandura, A. (1996). Social learning theory: Overview of Bandura's theory. Retrieved from http://condor.admin.ccny.cuny.edu/~hhartman/Overview%20of%20Bandura's%20Theory.htm (accessed February 21, 2014).

Barnes, R. (2013, June 24). Supreme Court sends Texas affirmative action plan back for further review. *The Washington Post*. Retrieved from http://articles.washington post.com/2013–06–24/politics/40157367_1_admissions-policies-grutter-justice-ruth-bader-ginsburg (accessed February 21, 2014).

Barnett, M. (2004). A qualitative analysis of family support and interaction among Black college students at an Ivy League University. *The Journal of Negro Education*, 73(1), 53–68.

Barr, M. J., Desler, M. K., & Associates (2000). *The handbook of student affairs administration*. San Francisco, CA: Jossey-Bass.

Bean, J. P., & Metzner, B. S. (1985). A conceptual model of nontraditional undergraduate student attrition. *Review of Educational Research*, 55(4), 485–540.

Bell, D. A. (1980). Brown v. Board of Education and the interest-convergence dilemma. *Harvard Law Review*, 93, 518–533.

Bensimon, E. M. (2005). Closing the achievement gap in higher education: An organizational learning perspective. *New Directions for Higher Education*, 131, 99–111.

Bensimon, E. M. (2007). The underestimated significance of practitioner knowledge in the scholarship of student success. *Review of Higher Education*, 30, 441–469.

Bensimon, E. M. (2011). The critical role of community college practitioners in the success of students of color. Symposium presented at the annual meeting of the Association for the Study of Higher Education, Council on Ethnic Participation, Charlotte, NC.

Bensimon, E. M., & Malcom, L. (Eds.) (2012). Introduction. In E. M. Bensimon & L. Malcom (Eds.), *Confronting equity issues on campus: Implementing the equity scorecard in theory and practice* (pp. 1–16). Sterling, VA: Stylus.

Bledsoe, T., & Rome, K. (2006). Student African American brotherhood. In M. J. Cuyjet (Ed.), *African American men in college* (pp. 24–46). San Francisco, CA: Jossey Bass.

Bonner II, F. (2010). *Academically gifted African American males in college*. Santa Barbara, CA: ABC-CLIO.

Bonner II, F. (2012). Standing in the intersection: Black, male, millennial college students. In R. T. Palmer & J. L. Wood (Eds.), *Black men in college. Implications for HBCUs and beyond*. (pp. 107–121). New York: Routledge.

Bonner II, F. (Ed.) (2014a). *Building on resilience: Models and frameworks of Black male success across the P-20 pipeline*. Sterling, VA: Stylus.

Bonner II, F. (2014b). *Frameworks and models of Black male success: A guide for P-12 and postsecondary educators*. Sterling, VA: Stylus.

Bonner II, F., & Bailey, K. W. (2006). Enhancing the academic climate for African American men. In M. J. Cuyjet (Ed.), *African American men in college* (pp. 24–46). San Francisco, CA: Jossey-Bass.

Bonous-Hammarth, M., & Boatsman, K. (1996). Satisfaction guaranteed? Predicting academic and social outcomes for African American college students. Paper presented at the Annual Conference of the American Educational Research Association, New York.

BPS. (2009a). *Beginning postsecondary students longitudinal study. First degree attained through 2009 by institutional sector level and control and (Black) and (male).* Washington, DC: National Center for Education Statistics.

BPS. (2009b). *Beginning postsecondary students longitudinal study. Student degree intentions by institutional sector level and control and (Black) and (male).* Washington, DC: National Center for Education Statistics.

Branch-Brioso, K. (2009). What will it take to increase Hispanics in STEM? Money, of course. *Diverse Education.* Retrieved from http://diverseeducation.com/cache/print.php?articleId=12347 (accessed January 6, 2014).

Bronfenbrenner, U. (1989). Ecological systems theory. In R. Vasta (Ed.), *Annal of child development* (pp. 187–249). Greenwich, CT: JAI.

Brown, C. (2006). The impact of campus activities on African American college men. In M. J. Cuyjet (Ed.), *African American men in college* (pp. 47–67). San Francisco, CA: Jossey Bass.

Burd, S. (2011). Budget cutters take aim at TRIO and Gear Up. New America Foundation. Retrieved from http://edmoney.newamerica.net/blogposts/2011/budget_cutters_take_aim_at_the_trio_and_gear_up_programs-49427 (accessed January 6, 2014).

Bush, E. C. (2004). *Dying on the vine: A look at African American student achievement in California community colleges* (Doctoral dissertation). Available from ProQuest Dissertations and Theses database (UMI No. 3115606).

Bush, E. C., & Bush, L. V. (2005). Black male achievement and the community college. *Black Issues in Higher Education*, 22(2), 44.

Bush, E. C., & Bush, L. V. (2010). Calling out the elephant: An examination of African American male achievement in community colleges. *Journal of African American Males in Education*, 1(1), 40–62.

Bush, L. V., & Bush, E. C. (2013a). Introducing African American male theory (AAMT). *Journal of African American Males in Education*, 4(1), 6–17.

Bush, L. V., & Bush, E. C. (2013b). God bless the child who got his own: Toward a comprehensive theory for African-American boys and men. *Western Journal of Black Studies*, 37(1), 1–13.

Campbell, D. B., & Fleming, J. (2000). Fear of success, racial identity, and academic achievement in Black male college students. *Community Review*, 18, 5–18.

Carey, K. (2008). *Graduation rate watch: Making minority student success a priority.* Washington, DC: Educational Sector.

Carr, K. M. (2013, June 8). Supreme Court signals the end for affirmative action as we know it. *Baltimore Sun.* Retrieved from http://articles.baltimoresun.com/2013–07–08/news/bs-ed-affirmative-action-20130708_1_regents-v-affirmative-action-academic-freedom (accessed February 21, 2014).

Carroll, J. (1988). Freshman retention and attrition factors at a predominantly Black urban community college. *Journal of College Student Development*, 29(1), 52–60.

CCSSE. (2014). *Aspirations to achievement: Men of color and community colleges.* Austin, TX: Community College Survey of Student Engagement.

Cokley, K. (2001). Gender differences among African American students in the impact of racial identity on academic psychosocial development. *Journal of College Student Development*, 42, 480–487.

Cokley, K. (2003). What do we know about the academic motivation of African American college students? Challenging the "anti-intellectual myth." *Harvard Educational Review*, 73, 524–558.

Cook, P. J., & Ludwig, J. (1998). The burden of "acting White": Do Black adolescents disparage academic achievement? In C. Jencks & M. Phillips (Eds.), *The Black–White test score gap* (pp. 375–400). Washington, DC: Brookings Institution Press.

Coppin Academy High School. (n. d.). Retrieved from www.baltimorecityschools.org/domain/4663 (accessed February 21, 2014).

Corbin, S. K., & Pruit, R. L. (1999). *Who am I? The development of the African American male identity.* New York: Teachers College.

Cross, W. E. (1991). *Shades of Black.* Philadelphia, PA: Temple University.

Cuyjet, M. J. (Ed.) (1997). Helping African American men succeed in college. *New Directions for Student Services*, 80. San Francisco, CA: Jossey-Bass.

Cuyjet, M. J. (Ed.) (2006). *African American men in college.* San Francisco, CA: Jossey-Bass.

Dancy, T. E. (2012). *The brother code: Manhood and masculinity among African American men in college.* Charlotte, NC: Information Age Publishing.

Dancy, T. E., & Brown, M. C. (2012). *African American males and education: Researching the convergence of race and identity*. Charlotte, NC: Information Age Publishing.

Darling-Hammond, L. (2000). Teacher quality and student achievement: A review of state policy evidence. *Educational Policy Analysis Archives*, 8(1). Retrieved from http://epaa.asu.edu/epaa/v8n1/ (accessed January 6, 2014).

Davis, J. E. (1994). College in Black and White: Campus environment and academic achievement of African American males. *The Journal of Negro Education*, 63, 620–633.

Davis, J. E. (2003). Early schooling and academic achievement of African American males. *Urban Education*, 38(5), 515–537.

Davis, R. J., & Palmer, R. T. (2010). The role and relevancy of postsecondary remediation for African American students: A review of research. *Journal of Negro Education*, 79(4), 503–520.

Digest of Education Statistics. (2011). Higher Education General Information Survey (HEGIS), "Fall Enrollment in Colleges and Universities" surveys, 1976 and 1980; Integrated Postsecondary Education Data System (IPEDS), "Fall Enrollment Survey" (IPEDS-EF:90); and IPEDS Spring 2001 through Spring 2011, Enrollment component. Washington, DC: U. S. Department of Education, National Center for Education Statistics.

Doubleday, J. (2013). With parents denied, students scramble at HBCUs. Retrieved from http://chronicle.com/article/Without-Federal-PLUS-Loans/142147/(accessed January 6, 2014).

Dowd, A. C., Pak, J. H., & Bensimon, E. M. (2013). The role of institutional agents in promoting transfer access. *Education Policy Analysis Archives*, 21(15), 2–38.

The Education Trust. (2009). The education trust challenge to key education leaders: Help close the teaching talent gap now. Retrieved from www.edtrust.org/dc/press-room/press-release/the-education-trust-issues-challenge-to-key-education-leaders-help-close (accessed June 2, 2014).

Edwards, M., Cangemi, J. P., & Kowalski, C. J. (1990). The college dropout and institutional responsibility. *Education*, 111(1), 107–116.

Entman, R. M. (1993). Framing: Toward clarification of a fractured paradigm. *Journal of Communication*, 43, 51–58.

Epps, E. G. (1995). Race, class, and educational opportunity: Trends in the sociology of education. *Sociological Forum*, 10(4), 593–608.

Esters, L. L., & Mosby, D. C. (2007). Disappearing acts: The vanishing Black male on community college campuses. *Diverse Issues in Higher Education*, 24(14), 45.

Feagin, J. R., Vera, H., & Imani, N. (1996). *The agony of education. Black students at White colleges and universities.* New York: Nikitah Publications.

Fisher v. University of Texas at Austin. (2013). 133 S. Ct. 2411.

Fleming, J. (1984). *Blacks in college: A comparative study of student success in Black and White institutions.* San Francisco, CA: Jossey-Bass.

Flores, A. (2007). Examining disparities in mathematics education: Achievement gap or opportunity gap? *High School Journal*, 91(1), 29–42.

Flowers, L. (2002). The impact of college racial composition on African American students' academic and social gains. Additional evidence. *Journal of College Student Development*, 43(3), 403–410.

Flowers, L. (2006). Effects of attending a 2-year institution on African American males' academic and social integration in the first year of college. *Teachers College Record*, 108(2), 267–286.

Ford, D. Y., Moore III, J. L., & Milner, H. R. (2005). Beyond colorblindness: A model of culture with implications for gifted education. *Roeper Review*, 27, 97–103.

Fordham, S., & Ogbu, J. U. (1986). Black students' school success: Coping with the "burden of acting White." *The Urban Review*, 18(3), 179–205.

Fries-Britt, S., & Turner, B. (2002). Uneven stories: Successful Black collegians at a Black and a White campus. *Review of Higher Education*, 25(3), 315–330.

Gamoran, A., Porter, A. C., Smithson, J., & White, P. A. (1997). Upgrading high school mathematics instruction: Improving learning opportunities for low-achieving, low-income youth. *American Evaluation and Policy Analysis*, 19(4), 325–338.

Garibaldi, A. M. (2007). The education status of African-American males in the 21st century. *Journal of Negro Education*, 76(3), 324–333.

Garvin, D. A. (1994). Building a learning organization. *Business Credit*, 96, 19–27.

Gasman, M. (2008). Minority-serving institutions: An historical backdrop. In M. Gasman, B. Baez, & C. S. Turner (Eds.), *Understanding minority-serving institutions* (pp. 18–27). Albany, NY: SUNY Press.

Gasman, M. (2013). *The changing faces of historically Black colleges and universities.* Center for Minority Serving Institutions (MSIs). University of Pennsylvania Graduate School of Education. Retrieved from www.gse.upenn.edu/pdf/cmsi/Changing_Face_HBCUs.pdf (accessed January 6, 2014).

Gasman, M., Baez, B., Drezner, N. D., Sedgwick, K., Tudico, C., & Schmid, J. M. (2007). Historically Black colleges and universities: Recent trends. *Academe*, 93(1), 69–78.

Gasman, M., & Bowman III, N. (2011). *A guide to fundraising at Historically Black Colleges and Universities: An all campus approach.* New York: Routledge.

Gasman, M., Lundy-Wagner, V., Ransom, T., & Bowman, N. (2010). Unearthing promise and potential: Our nation's historically Black colleges and universities. *ASHE Higher Education Report.* San Francisco, CA: Jossey-Bass.

General Accounting Office. (1995). *Higher education: Restructuring student aid could reduce low-income student dropout rate* (GAO/HEHS-95-48). Washington, DC: U. S. Government Printing Office.

Good, C., Aronson, J., & Inzlicht, M. (2003). Improving adolescents' standardized test performance: An intervention to reduce the effects of Stereotype Threat. *Journal of Applied Developmental Psychology*, 24, 645–662.

Green, P. (2000). African American men and the academy. In L. Jones (Ed.), *Brothers of the academy: Up and coming Black scholars earning our way in higher education* (pp. 3–22). Sterling, VA: Stylus.

Guba, E. G., & Lincoln, Y. S. (1994). Competing paradigms in qualitative research. In N. Denzin & Y. Lincoln (Eds.), *Handbook of qualitative research* (pp. 105–117). Thousand Oaks, CA: Sage.

Guiffrida, D. A. (2004). Friends from home: Asset and liability to African American students attending a predominantly White institution. *NASPA Journal*, 24(3), 693–708.

Guiffrida, D. A. (2005). Othermothering as a framework for understanding African American student definitions of student-centered faculty. *Journal of Higher Education*, 76(6), 701–723.

Guiffrida, D. A. (2006). Toward a cultural advancement of Tinto's theory. *Review of Higher Education*, 29(4), 451–472.

Hagedorn, S. L., Maxwell, W., & Hampton, P. (2001–2002). Correlates of retention for African-American males in the community college. *Journal of College Student Retention*, 3(3), 243–263.

Hale, J. E. (2001). *Learning while Black: Creating educational excellence for African American children*. Baltimore, MD: Johns Hopkins University Press.

Harbour, C. P., & Nagy, P. (2005). Assessing a state-mandated institutional accountability program: The perceptions of selected community college leaders. *Community College Journal of Research and Practice*, 29, 445–461.

Harper, S. R. (2004). The measure of a man: Conceptualizations of masculinity among high-achieving African American male college students. *Berkeley Journal of Sociology*, 48, 89–107.

Harper, S. R. (2005). Leading the way: Inside the experiences of high-achieving African American male students. *About Campus*, 10(1), 8–15.

Harper, S. R. (2006). *Black male students at public universities in the U. S.: Status, trends, and implications for policy, and practice*. Washington, DC: Joint Center for Political and Economic Studies.

Harper, S. R. (2009). Institutional seriousness concerning Black male student engagement: Necessary conditions and collaborative partnerships. In S. R. Harper & S. J. Quaye (Eds.), *Student engagement in higher education: Theoretical perspectives and practical approaches for diverse populations* (pp. 137–156). New York: Routledge.

Harper, S. R. (2010). An anti-deficit achievement framework for research on students of color in STEM. *New Directions for Institutional Research*, 148, 63–74.

Harper, S. R. (2012). *Black male student success in higher education: A report from the national Black male college achievement study*. Philadelphia, PA: University of Pennsylvania, Center for the Study of Race and Equity in Education.

Harper, S. R. (2014). (Re)setting the agenda for college men of color: Lessons learned from a 15-year movement to improve Black male student success. In R. A. Williams (Ed.), *Men of color in higher education: New foundations for developing models for success* (pp. 116–143). Sterling, VA: Stylus.

Harper, S. R., Carini, R. M., Bridges, B. K., & Hayek, J. (2004). Gender differences in student engagement among African American undergraduates at historically Black colleges and universities. *Journal of College Student Development*, 45(3), 271–284.

Harper, S. R., Davis, R. J., Jones, D. E., McGowan, B. L., Ingram, T. N., & Platt, C. S. (2011). Race and racism in the experiences of Black male resident assistants at predominantly White universities. *Journal of College Student Development*, 52(2), 180–200.

Harper, S. R., & Gasman, M. (2008). Consequences of conservatism: Black male undergraduates and the politics of historically Black colleges and universities. *Journal of Negro Education*, 77(4), 336–351.

REFERENCES

Harper, S. R., Harris III, F. (2012). *Men of color: A role for policymakers in improving the status of Black male students in U. S. higher education.* Washington, DC: Institute for Higher Education Policy.

Harper, S. R., & Kuykendall, J. A. (2012). Institutional efforts to improve Black male student achievement: A standards-based approach. *Change*, 44(2), 23–29.

Harper, S. R., & Nichols, A. H. (2008). Are they not all the same? Racial heterogeneity among Black male undergraduates. *Journal of College Student Development*, 49(3), 1–16.

Harper, S. R., & Quaye, S. J. (2007). Student organizations as venues for Black identity expression and development among African American male student leaders. *Journal of College Student Development*, 48(2), 127–144.

Harper, S. R., & Quaye, S. J. (Eds.) (2009). *Student engagement in higher education: Theoretical perspectives and practical approaches for diverse populations.* New York: Routledge.

Harper, S. R., & Wood, J. L. (Eds.) (2014). *Advancing Black male student success.* Sterling, VA: Stylus.

Harris III, F., Bensimon, E. M., & Bishop, R. (2010). The Equity Scorecard: A process for building institutional capacity to educate young men of color. In C. Edley, Jr. & J. Ruiz de Velasco (Eds.), *Changing places: How communities will improve the health of boys of color* (pp. 277–308). Berkeley, CA: University of California Press.

Harris III, F., & Harper, S. R. (2008). Masculinities go to community college: Understanding male identity socialization and gender role conflict. *New Directions for Community Colleges*, 142, 25–35.

Harris, III, F., Palmer, R. T., & Struve, L. E. (2011). "Cool posing" on campus: A qualitative study of masculinities and gender expression among Black men at a private research institution. *Journal of Negro Education*, 80(1), 47–62.

Harris III, F., & Wood, J. L. (in press). The Socio-Ecological Outcomes model: A framework for examining men of color's experiences and success in community colleges. *New Directions for Community Colleges.*

Herndon, M. K. (2003). Expressions of spirituality among African-American college males. *Journal of Men's Studies*, 12(1), 75–84.

Hoffman, M., Richmond, J., Morrow, J., & Salomone, K. (2003). Investigating "sense of belonging" in first-year college students. *Journal of College Student Retention*, 4, 227–256.

Holmes, S. L., Ebbers, L. H., Robinson, D. C., & Mugenda, A. G. (2007). Validating African American students at predominantly White institutions. In A. Seidman (Ed.), *Minority student retention* (pp. 79–96). Amityville, NY: Baywood.

hooks, b. (2004). *We real cool: Black men and masculinity.* New York: Routledge.

Howard, T. C. (2006). The forgotten link: The salience of PreK-12 education and culturally responsive pedagogy in creating access for African American students. In J. F. L. Jackson (Ed.), *Strengthening the African American educational pipeline* (pp. 17–36). New York: State University Press.

102

Howard-Hamilton, M. F. (1997). Theory to practice: Applying developmental theories relevant to African American men. *New Directions for Student Services*, 80, 17–30.

Hrabowski, F., Maton, K. I., & Greif, G. L. (1998). *Beating the odds: Raising academically successful African American males*. New York: Oxford University Press.

Hurtado, S., & Carter, D. F. (1997). Effects of college transition and perceptions of the campus racial climate on Latino students' sense of belonging. *Sociology of Education*, 70, 324–345.

Hurtado, S., Carter, D. F., & Spuler, A. (1996). Latino students' transition to college: Assessing difficulties and factors in successful college adjustment. *Research in Higher Education*, 37(2), 135–158.

Jackson, J. F. L., & Moore III, J. L. (2006). African American males in education: Endangered or ignored. *Teachers College Record*, 108(2), 201–205.

Jackson, J. F. L., & Moore III, J. L. (2008). The African American male crisis in education: A popular media infatuation or needed public policy response. *American Behavioral Science*, 51(7), 847–853.

Jain, D., Herrera, A., Bernal, S., & Solórzano, D. (2011). Critical race theory and the transfer function: Introducing a transfer receptive culture. *Community College Journal of Research and Practice*, 35(3), 252–266.

Johnson, D. R., Soldner, M., Leonard, J. B., Alvarez, P., Inkelas, K. K., Rowan-Kenyon, H., et al. (2007). Examining sense of belonging among first-year undergraduates from different racial/ethnic groups. *Journal of College Student Development*, 48(5), 525–542.

Journal of Blacks in Higher Education (2008). More Blacks are competing in advanced placement programs, but the racial scoring gap is widening. Retrieved from www.jbhe.com/features/59_apscoringgap.html (accessed February 21, 2014).

Kaltenbaugh, L. S., St. John, E. P., & Starkey, J. B. (1999). What differences does tuition make? An analysis of ethnic differences in persistence. *Journal of Student Financial Aid*, 29(2), 21–31.

Kaplin, W., & Lee, B. (2007). *The law of higher education*. San Francisco, CA: Jossey-Bass.

Kerlinger, F. N. (1986). *Behavioral research: A conceptual approach*. New York: Holt, Rinehart and Winston.

Kezar, A. (2005a). What do we mean by "learning" in the context of higher education? *New Directions for Higher Education*, 131, 49–59.

Kezar, A. (2005b). What campuses need to know about organizational learning and the learning organization. *New Directions for Higher Education*, 131, 7–22.

Kim, M., & Conrad, C. F. (2006). The impact of historically Black colleges and universities on the academic success of African American students. *Research in Higher Education*, 47, 399–427.

Kim, Y. M. (2011). *Minorities in higher education status: Twenty-fourth status report 2011 supplement*. Washington, DC: American Council on Education.

Kimbrough, W. M., & Harper, S. R. (2006). African American men at historically Black colleges and universities: Different environments, similar challenges. In M. J. Cuyjet (Ed.), *African American men in college* (pp. 189–209). San Francisco, CA: Jossey-Bass.

Kuh, G. D. (1987). A brief for incorporating organizational theory in student affairs preparation and research. Paper presented at the annual meeting of the Association for the Study of Higher Education, Baltimore, MD.

Kuh, G. D. (2003). What we're learning about student engagement from NSSE. *Change*, 35(2), 24–32.

Kuh, G. D., Kinzie, J., Buckley, J., Bridges, B., & Hayek, J. C. (2007). Piecing together the student success puzzle: Research, propositions, and recommendations. *ASHE Higher Education Report*, 32(5). San Francisco, CA: Jossey-Bass.

Ladson-Billings, G. (1997). It doesn't add up: African American students' mathematics achievement. *Journal for Research in Mathematics Education*, 28(6), 697–708.

LaVant, B., Anderson, J., & Tiggs, J. (1997). Retaining African American men through mentoring initiatives. *New Directions for Student Services*, 80, 43–53.

Lee, J. M. (2012). An examination of the participation of African American students in graduate education without public HBCUs. In R. T. Palmer, A. A. Hilton, & T. P. Fountaine (Eds.), *Black graduate education at historically Black colleges and universities* (pp. 61–82). Charlotte, NC: Information Age.

Levin, H. M., Belfield, C., Muennig, P., & Rouse, C. (2007). The public returns to public educational investments in African American males. *Economics of Educational Review*, 26, 700–709.

Lott, J. (2011) Testing the factorial invariance of the Black racial identity scale across gender. *Journal of College Student Development*, 52(2), 224–234.

Love, P., & Talbot, D. (1999). Defining spiritual development: A missing consideration for student affairs. *Journal of Student Affairs Research and Practice*, 26(4), 1164–1178.

Lundberg, C. A., & Schreiner, L. A. (2004). Quality and frequency of faculty–student interaction as predictors of learning: An analysis by student race/ethnicity. *Journal of College Student Development*, 45(5), 549–565.

Lundy, G. F. (2003). School resistance in American high schools: The role of race and gender in oppositional culture theory. *Evaluation and Research in Education*, 17(1), 6–27.

Lundy, G. F. (2005). Peer relations and school resistance: Does oppositional culture apply to race or to gender? *Journal of Negro Education*, 73(3), 233–245.

Lundy-Wagner, V. C., & Gasman, M. (2011). When gender issues are not just about women: Reconsidering Black men at historically Black colleges and universities. *Teachers College Record*, 113(5), 934–968.

Maestas, R., Vaquera, G. S., & Zehr, L. M. (2007). Factors impacting sense of belonging at a Hispanic-Serving Institution. *Journal of Hispanic Higher Education*, 6(3), 237–256.

Majors, R., & Billson, J. (1992). *Cool pose: The dilemmas of Black manhood in America.* New York: Touchstone.

Majors, R., Tyler, R., Peden, B., & Hall, R. (1994). Cool pose: A symbolic mechanism for masculine role enactment and coping by Black males. In R. Majors & J. U. Gordon (Eds.), *The American Black male: His present status and his future* (pp. 245–259). Chicago, IL: Nelson-Hall.

Marks, B. T. (2014, March 28). My brother's keeper: Black male success in higher education. Presented at the White House and Morehouse College Summit on Black males, Atlanta, GA.

Mason, H. P. (1994). *The relationships of academic, background, and environmental variables in the persistence of adult African American male students in an urban community college* (Doctoral dissertation). Available from ProQuest Dissertations and Theses database (UMI No. 9430242).

Mason, H. P. (1998). A persistence model for African American male urban community college students. *Community College Journal of Research and Practice, 22*(8), 751–760.

Mattis, J. S. (2000). African American women's definitions of spirituality and religiosity. *Journal of Black Psychology, 26*(1), 101–122.

Mattis, J. S. (2004). Spirituality and religion in African-American life. In R. L. Jones (Ed.), *Black psychology* (4th ed.) (pp. 93–115). Hampton, VA: Cobb & Henry.

Mayer, D. P., Mullens, J. E., & Moore, M. T. (2000). Monitoring school quality: An indicators report, NCES 2001–030. Washington, DC: National Center for Education Statistics. Retrieved from www.nces.ed.gov/pubs2001/2001030.pdf (accessed February 21, 2014).

Merriam, S. B. (1998). *Qualitative research and case study applications in education.* San Francisco, CA: Jossey-Bass.

Miller, D. K., & Mupinga, D. M. (2006). Similarities and differences between public and proprietary postsecondary 2-year technical institutions. *Community College Journal of Research and Practice, 30,* 565–577.

Mitchell, S. L., & Dell, D. M. (1992). The relationship between Black students' racial identity attitude and participation in campus organizations. *Journal of College Student Developments, 33*(1), 39–43.

Moody, J. (2012). *Faculty diversity: Removing the barriers* (2nd ed.). New York: Routledge.

Moore, F. L. (2000). The role of mentoring for the educated Black man. In L. Jones (Ed.), *Brothers of the academy: Up and coming Black scholars earning our way in higher education* (pp. 181–190). Sterling, VA: Stylus.

Moore III, J. L. (2001). Developing academic warriors: Things that parents, administrators, and faculty should know. In L. Jones (Ed.), *Retaining African Americans in higher education: Challenging paradigms for retaining students, faculty, and administrators* (pp. 77–90). Sterling, VA: Stylus.

Moore, III, J. L., Henfield, M. S., & Owens, D. (2008). African American males in special education: Their attitudes and perceptions toward high school counselors and school counseling services. *American Behavioral Scientist, 51,* 907–927.

Moore III, J. L., Madison-Colmore, O., & Smith, D. M. (2003). The prove-them-wrong syndrome: Voices from unheard African American males in engineering disciplines. *Journal of Men's Studies*, 12(1), 61–73.

Mosby, J. R. (2009). *From strain to success: A phenomenological study of the personal and academic pressures on African American male community college students* (Doctoral dissertation). Available from ProQuest Dissertations and Theses database (UMI No. 3368203).

Mullin, C. M. (2010). *Just how similar? Community colleges and the for-profit sector.* Washington, DC: American Association of Community Colleges.

Museus, S. D. (2008). Understanding the role of ethnic student organizations in facilitating cultural adjustment and membership among African American and Asian American college students. *Journal of College Student Development*, 59(6), 568–586.

Nasim, A., Roberts, A., Hamell, J. P., & Young, H. (2005). Non-cognitive predictors of academic achievement for African Americans across cultural contexts. *The Journal of Negro Education*, 74(4), 344–359.

National Center for Public Policy and Higher Education. (2011). *Policy alert: Affordability and transfer: Critical to increasing baccalaureate degree completion.* Retrieved from www.highereducation.org/reports/pa_at/index.shtml (accessed January 6, 2014).

Nelson, A. L. (2012). Crack down on parent PLUS loans. Retrieved from www.insidehighered.com/news/2012/10/12/standards-tightening-federal-plus-loans#sthash.WfZ5x2lG.dpbs (accessed June 2, 2014).

Nevarez, C., & Wood, J. L. (2010). *Community college leadership and administration: Theory, practice and change.* New York: Peter Lang.

Newman, C., Wood, J. L., & Harris III, F. (in press). Black males' masculinity and the impact on sense of belonging with faculty members in community college. *Journal of Negro Education.*

Nora, A., & Cabrera, A. F. (1996). The role of perceptions of prejudice and discrimination on the adjustment of minority students to college. *Journal of Higher Education*, 67(2), 119–148.

NPSAS. (2004). *Institution: sector by Race/ethnicity for Gender (Male). 2003–04 National Postsecondary Student Aid Study (NPSAS:04).* Washington, DC: U. S. Department of Education, National Center for Education Statistics.

NPSAS. (2012). *NPSAS institution sector (4 with multiple) by Race/ethnicity (with multiple) for Gender (Male).* Washington, DC: U. S. Department of Education, National Center for Education Statistics.

Oakes, J., Gamoran, A., & Page, R. N. (1992). Curriculum differentiation: Opportunities, outcome, and meanings. In P. W. Jackson (Ed.), *Handbook of research on curriculum* (pp. 570–608). New York: Macmillan.

Ogbu, J. U. (1991). Cultural diversity and school experience. In C. E. Walsh (Ed.), *Literacy as praxis: Culture, language, and pedagogy* (pp. 25–50). Norwood, NJ: Ablex.

Okech, A., & Harrington, R. (2002). The relationship between Black consciousness, self-esteem, and academic self-efficacy in African American men. *Journal of Psychology: Interdisciplinary and Applied*, 136, 214–224.

Ostrove, J. M. (2003). Belonging and wanting: Meanings of social class background for women's constructions of their college experience. *Journal of Social Issues*, 59, 771–784.

Ostrove, J. M., & Long, S. M. (2007). Social class and belonging: Implications for college adjustment. *The Review of Higher Education*, 30(4), 363–389.

Ostrove, J. M., Stewart, A. J., & Curtin, N. L. (2011). Social class and belonging: Implications for graduate students' career aspirations. *The Journal of Higher Education*, 82(6), 748–774.

Outcalt, C. L., & Skewes-Cox, T. E., (2002). Involvement, interaction, and satisfaction: The human environment at HBCUs. *Review of Higher Education*, 25(3), 331–347.

Pace, C. R. (1980). Measuring the quality of student effort. *Current Issues in Higher Education*, 2, 10–16.

Pace, C. R. (1984). *Measuring the quality of college student experiences: An account of the development and use of the College Student Experiences Questionnaire.* Los Angeles, CA: Higher Education Research Institute.

Pace, C. R. (1985). *The credibility of student self-reports.* Los Angeles, CA: Center for the Study of Evaluation, University of California.

Pace, C. R. (1990). *The undergraduates: A report of their activities and college experiences in the 1980s.* Los Angeles, CA: Center for the Study of Evaluation, UCLA Graduate School of Education.

Palmer, R. T., & Davis, R. J. (2012). "Diamond in the rough": The impact of a remedial program on college access and opportunity for Black males at an historically Black institution. *Journal of College Student Retention*, 13(4), 407–430.

Palmer, R. T., Davis, R. J., & Hilton, A. A. (2009). Exploring challenges that threaten to impede the academic success of academically underprepared African American male collegians at an HBCU. *Journal of College Student Development*, 50(4), 429–445.

Palmer, R. T., Davis, R. J., & Maramba, D. C. (2011). The impact of family support on the success of Black men at an historically Black university: Affirming the revision of Tinto's theory. *Journal of College Student Development*, 52(5), 577–593.

Palmer, R. T., Davis, R. J., & Thompson, T. (2010). Theory meets practice: HBCU initiatives that promote academic success among African Americans in STEM. *Journal of College Student Development*, 51(4), 440–443.

Palmer, R. T., & Dubord, Z. (2013). Achieving success: A model of success for Black men in STEM at community colleges. In R. T. Palmer & J. L. Wood (Eds.), *Community colleges and STEM: Examining underrepresented racial and ethnic minorities* (pp. 193–208). New York: Routledge.

Palmer, R. T., & Gasman, M. (2008). "It takes a village to raise a child": The role of social capital in promoting academic success for African American men at a Black college. *Journal of College Student Development*, 49(1), 52–70.

Palmer, R. T., & Maramba, D. C. (2011). Using a tenet of critical theory to explain the African American male achievement disparity. *Education and Urban Society*, 43(4), 431–450.

Palmer, R. T., & Maramba, D. C. (2012). Creating conditions of mattering to enhance persistence for Black males at an historically Black University. *Spectrum: Journal on Black Men*, 1(1), 95–120.

Palmer, R. T., Maramba, D. C., & Dancy, T. E. (2013). The magnificent "MILE": Impacting Black male retention and persistence at an HBCU. *Journal of College Student Retention*, 15(1), 65–72.

Palmer, R. T., & Strayhorn, T. L. (2008). Mastering one's own fate: Non-cognitive factors with the success of African American males at an HBCU. *National Association of Student Affairs Professionals Journal*, 11(1), 126–143.

Palmer, R. T., & Wood, J. L. (Eds.). (2012). *Black men in college: Implications for HBCUs and beyond*. New York: Routledge.

Palmer, R. T., Wood, J. L., Dancy, T. E., & Strayhorn, T. (2014). Black male collegians: Increasing access, retention, and persistence in higher education. *ASHE-Higher Education Report Series*. San Francisco, CA: Jossey-Bass.

Palmer, R. T., & Young E. M. (2009). Determined to succeed: Salient factors that foster academic success for academically unprepared Black males at a Black college. *Journal of College Student Retention*, 10(4), 465–482.

Parker, M., & Flowers, L. A. (2003). The effects of racial identity on academic, achievement and perceptions of campus connectedness on African American students at predominantly White institutions. *College Student Affairs Journal*, 22(2), 180–194.

Pascarella, E. T., Edison, M., Nora, A., Hagedorn, L. S., & Terenzini, P. T. (1998). Does community college attendance influence students' educational plans? *Journal of College Student Development*, 39, 179–193.

Patton, L. (2006). The voice of reason: A qualitative examination of Black student perceptions of Black cultural centers. *Journal of College Student Development*, 47(6), 628–646.

Perna, L. W. (2006). Understanding the relationship between information about college costs and financial aid and students' college related behaviors. *American Behavioral Scientist*, 49, 1620–1635.

Perna, L. W., & Jones, A. P. (2013). *The state of college access and completion: improving college success for students from underrepresented groups*. New York: Routledge.

Poole, J. S. (2006). *Predictors of persistent Black male students' commitment to rural Mississippi two-year public institutions* (Doctoral dissertation). Available from ProQuest Dissertations and Theses database (UMI No. 3211245).

Pope, M. L. (2006). Meeting the challenges to African American men at community colleges. In M. J. Cuyjet (Ed.), *African American men in college* (pp. 210–236). San Francisco, CA: Jossey-Bass.

Ray, K., Carly, S. M., & Brown, D. (2009). Power of mentoring African American males in community colleges. In H. T. Frierson, W. Pearson, Jr., & J. H. Wyche (Eds.), *Black American males in higher education: Diminishing, proportions* (pp. 271–297). Bingley, UK: Emerald Group.

Reid, K. (2013). Understanding the relationship among racial identity, self-efficacy, institutional integration and academic achievement of Black males attending research universities. *The Journal of Negro Education*, 82(1), 75–93.

Rendón, L. I. (1994). Validating culturally diverse students: Toward a new model of learning and student development. *Innovative Higher Education*, 19(1), 33–51.

Rendón, L. I., Jalomo, R. E., & Nora, A. (2000). Theoretical considerations in the study of minority student retention in higher education. In J. M. Braxton (Ed.), *Reworking the student departure puzzle* (pp. 127–156). Nashville, TN: Vanderbilt University Press.

Rideaux, L. (2004). *African American male participation at Tomball College: Barriers, outreach, and retention* (Doctoral dissertation). Available from ProQuest Dissertations and Theses database (UMI No. 3150598).

Riegg, C. S. (2006). *The economics of two-year college education: Essays on community colleges and proprietary schools* (Unpublished Doctoral dissertation). University of California, Los Angeles.

Riggins, R. K., McNeal, C., & Herndon, M. K. (2008). The role of spirituality among African-American college students attending a historically Black university. *College Student Journal*, 42(1), 70–81.

Robinson, T. L., & Howard-Hamilton, M. F. (1994). An Afrocentric paradigm: Foundations for a healthy self-image and healthy interpersonal relationships. *Journal of Mental Health Counseling*, 16, 327–339.

Rooks, N. M. (2013). For Black students, college degrees are separate and unequal. The Chronicle of Higher Education. Retrieved from http://chronicle.com/blogs/conversation/2013/07/10/for-black-students-college-degrees-are-separate-and-unequal/ (accessed February 21, 2014).

Rosas, M., & Hamrick, F. A. (2002). Postsecondary enrollment and academic decision making: Family influences on women college students of Mexican descent. *Equity & Excellence in Education*, 35(1), 59–69.

Ross, M. (1998). *Success factors of young African American males at a historically Black college*. Westport, CT: Bergin and Garvey.

St. John, E. P. (2002). *The access challenge: Rethinking the causes of the new inequality* (policy issues report). Bloomington, IN: Indiana University, Education Policy Center.

St. John, E. P. (2003). *Refinancing the college dream: Access, equal opportunity, and justice for taxpayers*. Baltimore, MD: Johns Hopkins University.

St. John, E. P., & Starkey, J. B. (1995). An alternative to net price: Assessing the influence of prices and subsidies on within-year persistence. *Journal of Higher Education*, 66(2), 156–186.

Sax, L. J., Bryant, A. N., & Harper, C. E. (2005). The differential effects of student–faculty interaction on college outcomes for women and men. *Journal of College Student Development*, 46(6), 642–659.

Schoenfeld, A. H. (2002). Making mathematics work for all children: Issues of standards, testing, and equity. *Educational Researcher*, 31(1), 13–35.

Scott, J. A. (2012). "Reaching out to my brothers": Improving the retention of low-income Black men at historically Black colleges and universities: A critical review of the literature. In R. T. Palmer & J. L. Wood (Eds.), *Black men in college: Implications for HBCUs and beyond* (pp. 57–70). New York: Routledge.

Sevilla, C. G., Ochave, J. A., Punsalan, T. G., Regala, B. P., & Uriarte, G. G. (1992). *Research methods* (rev. ed.). Quezon City, Phillipines: REX.

Smedley, B. D., Myers, H. F., & Harrell, S. P. (1993). Minority-status stresses and the college adjustment of ethnic minority freshmen. *Journal of Higher Education*, 64(4), 434–452.

Solórzano, D. G. (1998). Critical race theory, racial and gender microaggressions, and the experiences of Chicana and Chicano scholars. *International Journal of Qualitative Studies in Education*, 11, 121–136.

Solórzano, D. G., & Ornelas, A. (2002). A critical race analysis of advanced placement classes: A case of educational inequality. *Journal of Latinos and Education*, 1(4), 215–229.

Solórzano, D. G., & Villalpando, O. (1998). Critical race theory: Marginality and the experience of students of color in higher education. In C. A. Torres, & T. R. Mitchell (Eds.), *Sociology of education: Emerging perspectives* (pp. 211–224). New York: State University of New York Press.

Spady, W. G. (1970). Dropouts from higher education: An interdisciplinary review and synthesis. *Interchange*, 1, 64–85.

Starobin, S. S., Jackson, D., & Laanan, F. S. (2012). Model programs for STEM student success at minority serving two-year colleges. In R. T. Palmer, D. C. Maramba, & M. Gasman (Eds.) (pp. 59–71). *Fostering success of ethnic and racial minorities in STEM*. New York: Routledge.

Steele, C. (1997). A threat in the air: How stereotypes shape intellectual identity and performance. *American Psychologist*, 52(6), 613–629.

Stevens, C. D. (2006). *Skating the zones: African-American male students at a predominantly White community college* (Unpublished Doctoral Dissertation). New York University, New York.

Strayhorn, T. L. (2008). The role of supportive relationships in facilitating African American males' success in college. *NASPA Journal*, 45(1), 26–48.

Strayhorn, T. L. (2010). When race and gender collide: Social and cultural capital's influence on the academic achievement of African American and Latino males. *Review of Higher Education*, 33(3), 307–332.

Strayhorn, T. L. (2011). Traits, commitments, and college satisfaction among Black American community college students. *Community College Journal of Research and Practice*, 35(6), 437–453.

Strayhorn, T. L. (2012). *College students' sense of belonging: A key to educational success for all students.* New York: Routledge.

Strayhorn, T. L. (Ed.) (2013). *Living at the intersections: Social identities and Black collegians.* Charlotte, NC: Information Age Publishing.

Strayhorn, T. L., & Terrell, M. C. (Eds.) (2010). *The evolving challenges of Black college students: New insights for policy, practice and research.* Sterling, VA: Stylus.

Sutton, E. M. (2006). Developmental mentoring of African American college men. In M. J. Cuyjet (Ed.), *African American men in college* (pp. 95–111). San Francisco, CA: Jossey-Bass.

Swail., W. S., Redd, K. E., & Perna, L. W. (2003). Retaining minority students in higher education: A framework for success. *ASHE ERIC Higher Education Report*, 30(2). San Francisco, CA: Jossey Bass.

Tate, F. W. (2008). The politics economy of teacher quality in school mathematics: African American males, opportunity, structures, and method. *American Behavioral Scientist*, 51(7), 953–971.

Taylor, C. M., & Howard-Hamilton, M. F. (1995). Student involvement and racial identity attitudes among African American males. *Journal of College Student Development*, 36, 330–336.

Terenzini, P. T., Springer, L., Pascarella, E. T., & Nora. A. (1995). Academic and out-of-class influences on students' intellectual orientations. *The Review of Higher Education*, 19, 23–44.

Thompson, G. L., Warren, S., & Carter, L. (2004). It's not my fault: Predicting high school teachers who blame parents and students for students' low achievement. *High School Journal*, 87(3), 5–14.

Tierney, W. (1992). An anthropological analysis of student participation in college. *Journal of Higher Education*, 63, 603–618.

Tinto, V. (1975). Dropouts from higher education: A theoretical synthesis of recent research. *Review of Educational Research*, 45(1), 89–125.

Tinto, V. (1987). *Leaving college: rethinking the causes and cures of student attrition* (2nd ed.). Chicago, IL: University of Chicago Press.

Tinto, V. (1988). Stages of student departure: Reflections on the longitudinal character of student leaving. *Journal of Higher Education*, 59(4), 438–455.

Tinto, V. (1993). *Leaving college: Rethinking the causes and cures of student attrition* (2nd ed.). Chicago, IL: University of Chicago Press.

111

Titus, M. A. (2006). Understanding the influence of the financial context of institutions on student persistence at four-year colleges and universities. *Journal of Higher Education*, 77(2), 353–375.

Tracey, T. J., & Sedlacek, W. K. (1987). *A comparison of White and Black student academic success using noncognitive variables: A Lisrel analysis* (Research Report 6–87). College Park, MD: University of Maryland.

Turner, C. S. (1988). *Organizational determinants of the transfer of Hispanic students from two- to four-year colleges* (Unpublished Doctoral Dissertation). Stanford University, California.

Turner, C. S. (1990). A California case study: Organizational determinants of the transfer of Hispanic students from two- to four-year colleges in the bay area. *Metropolitan Education*, 6, 1–24.

Turner, C. S. (1992). It takes two to transfer: Relational networks and educational outcomes. *Community College Review*, 19(4), 27–33.

Turner, C. S. (1994). Guests in someone else's house: Students of color. *The Review of Higher Education*, 17(4), 355–370.

Turner, C. S., & Fryer, T. W., Jr. (1990). The transfer status of non-transfer students. *Community / Junior College Quarterly of Research and Practice*, 14(3), 213–226.

Tyson, K., Darity W., & Castellino, D. R. (2005). It's not "a Black thing": Understanding the burden of acting White and other dilemmas of high achievement. *American Sociological Review*, 70, 582–605.

United States Government Accountability Office. (2011). Postsecondary education: Student outcomes vary at for-profit, nonprofit, and public schools (GAO-12–143). Washington, DC: U. S. GAO. Retrieved from: www.gao.gov/assets/590/586738.pdf (accessed February 21, 2014).

U. S. Census. (2000). *Projections of the resident population by age, sex, race, and Hispanic origin: 1999 to 2100*. Washington, DC: Author.

U. S. Census Bureau. (2012). *The 2012 statistical abstract: The national data book. Table 233: Mean earnings by highest degree earned (2009)*. Washington, DC: U. S. Department of Commerce, Census Bureau.

U. S. Commission on Civil Rights. (2009). *Minorities in special education*. Washington, DC: Author.

Valbrun M. (2010). Black males missing from college campuses. *America's Wire*. Retrieved from: http://americaswire.org/drupal7/?q=content/black-males-missing-college-campuses (accessed June 2, 2014).

Visher, M. G., & Teres, J. (2011). *Breaking new ground: An impact study of career-focused learning communities at Kingsborough Community College*. New York: MDRC.

Watson, L. (2006). The role of spirituality and religion in the experiences of African American male college students. In M. J. Cuyjet (Ed.), *African American men in college* (pp. 112–127). San Francisco, CA: Jossey Bass.

Weddle-West, K., Hagan, W. H., & Norwood, K. M. (2013). Impact of college environments on the spiritual development of African American students. *Journal of College Student Development*, 54(3), 299–314.

Wei, C. C., & Carroll, C. D. (2004). *A decade of undergraduate student aid: 1989–90 to 1999–2000.* Washington, DC: National Center for Education Statistics.

Weiss, J. M., Visher, M. G., Teres, J., & Schneider, E. (2010, August). Learning communities for students in developmental reading: An impact study at Hillsborough community college. *National Center for Postsecondary Research: NCPR Brief*, 1–4.

Wood, J. L. (2008) Ethical dilemmas in African-American faculty representation. *Journal of Education Policy*. Retrieved from: https://www4.nau.edu/cee/jep/journalterms.aspx?term=1&year=2008 (accessed February 21, 2014).

Wood, J. L. (2010). *African American males in the community college: Towards a model of academic success* (Unpublished Doctoral Dissertation). Arizona State University, Tempe.

Wood, J. L. (2011, August 5). Laying the groundwork: Black male programs and initiatives in community colleges. *Community College Times*. Retrieved from www.community collegetimes.com (accessed January 6, 2014).

Wood, J. L. (2012a). Leaving the two-year college: Predictors of Black male collegian departure. *The Journal of Black Studies*, 43(3), 303–326.

Wood, J. L. (2012b). Black males in the community college: Using two national datasets to examine academic and social integration. *Journal of Black Masculinity*, 2(2), 56–88.

Wood, J. L. (2012c). Examining academic variables affecting the persistence and attainment of Black male collegians: A focus on performance and integration in the community college. *Race Ethnicity and Education* (doi: 10.1080/13613324. 2012.733687).

Wood, J. L. (2013). The same . . . but different: Examining background characteristics among Black males in public two-year colleges. *Journal of Negro Education*, 82(1), 47–61.

Wood, J. L. (2014). Apprehension to engagement in the classroom: Perceptions of Black males in the community college. *International Journal of Qualitative Studies in Education*, 27(6), 785–803.

Wood, J. L., & Essien-Wood, I. R. (2012). Capital Identity Projection: Understanding the psychosocial effects of capitalism on Black male community college students. *Journal of Economic Psychology*, 33(3), 984–995.

Wood, J. L., & Harris III, F. (2012, November). *Examining factors that influence men of color's success in community colleges.* Paper presented at the annual meeting of the Council on Ethnic Participation, Association for the Study of Higher Education, Las Vegas, NV.

Wood, J. L., & Harris III, F. (2013). The community college survey of men: An initial validation of the instrument's non-cognitive outcomes construct. *Community College Journal of Research and Practice*, 37, 333–338.

113

Wood, J. L., & Hilton, A. A. (2012). A metasynthesis of literature on Black males: An overview of 40 years of policy recommendations. In A. A. Hilton, J. L. Wood, & C. W. Lewis (Eds.), *Black males in postsecondary education: Examining their experiences in diverse institutional contexts* (pp. 5–28). Charlotte, NC: Information Age.

Wood, J. L., Hilton, A. A., & Lewis, C. (2011). Black male collegians in public two-year colleges: Student perspectives on the effect of employment on academic success. *National Association of Student Affairs Professionals Journal*, 14(1), 97–110.

Wood, J. L., & Ireland, M. Y. (2014). Supporting Black male community college success: Determinants of faculty–student engagement. *Community College Journal of Research and Practice*, 38(2–3), 154–165.

Wood, J. L., & Jones, T. K. (in press). Black males' perceptions of the work–college balance: The impact of employment on academic success in the community college. *Journal of Men's Studies*.

Wood, J. L., & Palmer, R. T. (2012). Innovative initiatives and recommendations for practice and future research: Enhancing the status of Black Men at HBCUs and beyond. In R. T. Palmer & J. L. Wood (Eds.), *Black men in college. Implications for HBCUs and beyond* (pp. 176–196). New York: Routledge.

Wood, J. L., & Palmer, R. T. (2014). The likelihood of transfer for Black males in community colleges: Examining the effects of engagement using multilevel, multinomial modeling. *Journal of Negro Education*, 82(3), 272–287.

Wood, J. L., & Turner, C. S. V. (2011). Black males and the community college: Student perspectives on faculty and academic success. *Community College Journal of Research & Practice*, 35, 135–151.

Wood, J. L., & Vasquez Urias, M. (2012). Community college vs. proprietary school outcomes: Student satisfaction among minority males. *Community College Enterprise*, 18(2), 83–100.

Wood, J. L., & Williams, R. C. (2013). Persistence factors for Black males in community college: An examination of background, academic, social, and environmental variables. *Spectrum: A Journal on Black Men*, 1(2), 1–28.

Yes We Can: The Schott 50 State Report on Public Education and Black Males. (2010). Retrieved from http://blackboysreport.org/bbr2010.pdf (accessed January 6, 2014).

Yosso, T. J. (2005). Whose culture has capital? A critical race theory discussion of community cultural wealth. *Race Ethnicity and Education*, 8(1), 69–91.

Index

117

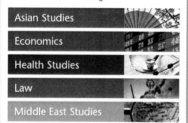